MARGARET DRABBLE:
A Reader's Guide

MARGARET DRABBLE:
A Reader's Guide

by

Valerie Grosvenor Myer

VISION PRESS · LONDON
ST. MARTIN'S PRESS · NEW YORK

Vision Press Ltd.
c/o Vine House Distribution
Waldenbury, North Common
Chailey, E. Sussex BN8 4DR

and

St. Martin's Press, Inc.
175 Fifth Avenue
New York
N.Y. 10010

ISBN (UK) 0 85478 187 0
ISBN (US) 0 312 06104 8

British Library Cataloguing-in-Publication Data
Myer, Valerie Grosvenor
    Margaret Drabble: a reader's guide—(Critical
    studies series)
    I. Title   II. Series
    823.914
    ISBN 0-85478-187-0

Library of Congress Cataloging-in-Publication Data
Myer, Valerie Grosvenor.
    Margaret Drabble: a reader's guide/ Valerie Grosvenor Myer.
    (Critical studies series)
    ISBN 0-312-06104-8
    1. Drabble, Margaret, 1939–   —Criticism and interpretation—
    I. Title.   II. Series.
    PR6054.R25275   1991
    823'.914—dc20   91-10737
                                                                        CIP

Printed and bound in Great Britain by
Billing & Sons, Worcester.
Typeset by Galleon Photosetting,
Ipswich, Suffolk.
MCMLXLI

Contents

'A real literary interest is an interest in man, society and civilization and its boundaries cannot be drawn.'

—F. R. Leavis, *The Common Pursuit* (1952)

'What are the critics to me?'

—Margaret Drabble, *Weekend Guardian*, 14–15 October 1989

This book is dedicated to Dr. Alice Heim, *who asked why I wasted my time on 'a lightweight like Margaret Drabble'.*

Acknowledgements

I am grateful to Margaret Drabble and her agents, the Fraser and Dunlop Group, for permission to quote from her works; to the British Council for permission to quote from my recorded interview with her; to Methuen and Co. for permission to quote from Joanne V. Creighton's *Margaret Drabble* (1985); and to Olga Kenyon for permission to quote from her books, *Women Novelists Today* (Brighton: Harvester Press, 1988) and *Women Writers Talk* (Oxford: Lennard Publishing, 1989). Other permissions have been sought.

My thanks are due to Nora Crook for reading Chapter 6 and making valuable suggestions.

Foreword

The conditions under which I wrote this book, in 1990, are very different from those under which I wrote my first, *Margaret Drabble: Puritanism and Permissiveness*, in 1974. At that time, Drabble had a large, enthusiastic readership in Britain, but was hardly known in America. In Britain she won awards, but it was not the fashion to take her seriously: I have heard her work dismissed as 'Tampax literature'. Although gynaecology features in Drabble's books, her treatment is restrained compared to that of later feminist writers. The climate in which I wrote was one in which critics (usually male) were scornful. Publishers reacted to the idea of a book on Drabble with derision: one or two of the rejection slips are in the collection of Dr. Nora Foster Stovel at the University of Alberta, Canada. My intention, naïve as it may appear in retrospect, was to establish that Drabble was a serious writer, a writer of quality, with the gifts of social observation, satiric wit, compassion and a coherent metaphysic. My book focussed on Drabble's concern with the soul of man and the residues of British puritanism. I had no models, no authorities, no advice (Drabble herself politely declined any connexion with the work). Drabble's novels were uncharted territory where I wandered alone, making my own discoveries.

My book received scant notice in Britain. Claire Tomalin, then literary editor of the *New Statesman*, refused to review it because it came 'too soon', though Drabble had published six novels and a book on Wordsworth. Then came the feminist movements of the '70s and Drabble attracted shoals of transatlantic interviewers, commentators and analysts. ('Drabble scholarship' remains largely an American phenomenon.) But, rather to my surprise, I find that critics have generally absorbed and acknowledged my book. So my original intention of updating it has become inappropriate. The present book is shaped by the gaps, as I see them, in the work of previous commentators, myself included.

Early reviewers spotted something special: the richness, variety and disagreement evinced by Drabble studies is surely proof of distinction. Comparison with Jane Austen gives way to comparison with George Eliot. While it is never fair to consider one writer in terms of another's achievement, there can be little doubt today that in her coherent vision of the human condition, in her intellectual power, moral analysis and bardic voice, Drabble fulfils the conditions of greatness.

V.G.M.
Cambridge, 1990

Introduction

Margaret Drabble is now a world figure, translated into sixteen languages, the subject of innumerable doctoral theses. She is author of (at the time of writing) eleven novels, short stories, plays, a biography and various books of commentary and criticism; and editor of the *Oxford Companion to English Literature*. The purpose of this study is to look at the way she fits into the tradition of the English novel and represents a particular strand in British society. Despite the proliferation of academic theses worldwide, and the fact that she has won several literary prizes and an honorary doctorate from the University of Sheffield, her home town, has been honoured with a C.B.E.[1] and invitations to lunch at Buckingham Palace, reviewers tend to be grudging. She is still occasionally dismissed as 'a woman's writer'. Yet her development as a writer over nearly thirty years has reflected much that is significant in British life.

Her first novel, *A Summer Birdcage*, appeared in 1963. In a famous poem, *Annus mirabilis*, the British poet Philip Larkin (1922–85) wrote memorably,

> Sexual intercourse began
> In 1963
> Between the end of the Chatterley ban
> And the Beatles' first L.P.

Larkin was, of course, exaggerating, but there is a germ of truth in his words: the trial of D. H. Lawrence's novel, *Lady Chatterley's Lover* (1928), in 1960 had considerable social repercussions. Lawrence had used 'four-letter words', previously regarded as obscene and unprintable. Larkin himself wrote a poem which began, 'They fuck you up, your mum and dad . . .' without any censorship of the taboo word. Sex, previously unmentioned, was open to public discussion,

13

endlessly. The result of the trial, which meant the book could be freely purchased and read in paperback at the price of 3s.6d. (17.5p) led, indirectly, to a flood of pornography and the coarsening of speech in public. The unsayable came to be said on all sorts of occasions previously unthinkable. This increased freedom of speech was paralleled by increased toleration of sexual behaviour formerly frowned upon; the biggest change was that young people lived openly together and produced children outside marriage. These developments attracted the label 'the permissive society'. 1963 was also the year Betty Friedan, an American, published *The Feminine Mystique*, a seminal book in Western feminism. It demonstrated that marriage and motherhood did not always bring happiness and fulfilment; despite propaganda to the contrary, they often brought on boredom, frustration and neurosis. Margaret Drabble first gained popular recognition as the novelist of the 'graduate wife', her career expectations dwindled down to washing nappies, chasing 'bits of soggy wet cotton' (*The Garrick Year*, 1964). A scholar at Newnham College, Cambridge, Drabble took a starred first[2] in the Tripos examinations and married an actor. At Cambridge she had earned a reputation as a gifted actress. But although she went on the stage, she only understudied stars like Vanessa Redgrave and Judi Dench, and the *longueurs* of the dressing room led to her writing. She became pregnant earlier than intended, but as she writes in *The Garrick Year*, the motherhood she had dreaded 'turned out to be one of my greatest joys'.

She was also the heir of the Puritan tradition. Professor Richard Hoggart, author of another seminal British book, *The Uses of Literacy* (1957), giving evidence for the defence at the Chatterley trial, described Lawrence's novel as 'highly virtuous and, if anything, puritanical'. The word 'puritanical' is often used to describe a mean, rigid, punitive morality. Under pressure, Professor Hoggart offered his own definition:

> Many people do live their lives under a misapprehension of the meaning of the word 'puritanical'. This is the way in which language decays. In England today and for a long time the word 'puritanical' has been extended to mean somebody who is against anything which is pleasurable, particularly sex.

The proper meaning of it, to a literary man or to a linguist, is somebody who belongs to the tradition of British puritanism generally, and the distinguishing feature of that is an intense sense of responsibility for one's conscience. In this sense the book is puritanical.[3]

And in this sense, Drabble, too, is puritanical. Americans, particularly feminists, generally fail to understand the tradition in which Drabble, a nonconformist socialist, has her being. Her background is one of conscientious striving: her mother, Marie Bloor, came from the Methodist working class, and was the first member of her family to go to university. Like her three daughters, she went to Newnham College, nursery of many British women novelists.[4] Marie Bloor glimpsed Edith Sitwell on a visit to the college, in the corridor. Marie's background emerges in *Jerusalem the Golden* (1967), *The Needle's Eye* (1972) and *The Realms of Gold* (1975). Marie's husband, John Drabble, who later became a judge, was the son of parents who owned a sweet factory. He made his own way to Cambridge University. In a newspaper interview, Margaret Drabble said her parents had protected her and her sisters and brother from the 'culture shock' experienced by her provincial grammar school parents on entering the then aristocratic world of Cambridge University: 'They couldn't afford *not* to spend money on our education.' Margaret Drabble has said that her maternal grandmother made her mother's childhood 'a misery'. This grim (but not untypical) British child-rearing ethos appears in *Jerusalem the Golden*. The critic Nora Stovel, in a private letter to me, has opined that such a background is 'too dreadful to be true', but unfortunately such mean parenting was, until recently, common in the lower middle class, particularly among northerners and nonconformists. A different kind of parental coldness, amounting perhaps to neglect along the lines of Dickens's Mrs. Jellyby,[5] is shown in *The Millstone* (1965), where the parents are socialist intellectuals concerned with changing the world, but keeping an emotional distance from their own daughter, refusing to intrude on her privacy. These parents represent the bourgeoisie into which the Drabble parents climbed. Marie retained her Yorkshire accent all her life and, despite her charm and humour, she suffered for years from social diffidence and depression, eventually alleviated by drugs, and her pride in the success of her children was not untinged with rivalry. After the parents were converted to the Quaker religion, the girls went to the Mount, a Quaker boarding school in York. Quakers, or the Society of Friends, as they prefer to be called, have no formulated creed, no liturgy, priesthood or sacrament. They give women an equal place with men in church organization. The emphasis is on personal responsibility, the inner light, quiet meditation and examination of the conscience, also a Methodist tradition. The Methodist morality often includes strict Sunday Observance, forbids drinking, gambling and, in extreme forms, theatrical entertainment or make-up. Drabble's biography of Arnold Bennett analyses this important inheritance. Methodism and egalitarian socialism historically go together: it is a commonplace that the Labour party drew its organization and rhetoric from the self-regulating Methodist chapels. Yet along with egalitarianism went a belief in striving, in self-improvement, a contradiction which causes much soul-searching among British intellectual socialists, many of whom are hostile to the idea of competition in any form, believing society should be organized to encourage co-operation. This conflict is played out in Drabble's novels, in particular *The Millstone* and *The Waterfall* (1969) where the heroine/narrator talks of 'the guilt of winning'. The guru of British socialists in Drabble's formative years was R. H. Tawney, author of *Religion and the Rise of Capitalism* (1926), a seminal book which we were required to read on the English undergraduate course at Newnham, taught under the influence of Dr. F. R. Leavis.[6] Its imagery pervades *The Waterfall* and many of its assumptions underlie Drabble's earlier work. Her sister, novelist A. S. Byatt, has said that in their household it was assumed all decent people voted Labour. British socialism owes more to Fabianism and William Morris than to Marx and Engels. It has less to do with protest than meliorism, the commitment to steady social improvement. For some thirty years its economics were Keynesian.[7]

Like other Newnham novelists such as Hilary Bailey and A. S. Byatt, Drabble has complained that the influence of Leavis's fastidiousness and exclusive emphasis on what he considered to be excellence was inhibiting to creativity. A generation of students from Leavis's period trembled before they dared set pen to paper for fear of the great man's wrath. Some were nervous of being caught admiring anything which might be condemned as second-rate, let alone writing it. Drabble has written to the *Times Literary Supplement* about this fear of being condemned as 'a minor writer'. She has repeatedly said she is not interested in writing 'experimental' or 'modernist novels'; she has declared her allegiance[8] to what Henry James dismissed as 'loose baggy monsters', sprawling naturalistic social narratives. Taken as a whole, her *oeuvre* weighs up the new morality against the old, incorporating the viewpoint of the intellectual socialist wife and mother. She is sometimes dismissed as 'a Hampstead novelist' because her characters live in or around that fashionable and expensive area of London, inhabited by rich socialists and famous writers like herself. She is, although socially privileged by education and career, in the tradition of radical dissent, religious and political. This is typical of a certain strand among England's upper middle class. Its memorial is *The Millstone*, which explores the tensions inherent in this position. But, whatever their politics, women readers, in very different circumstances, report their excitement in discovering Drabble's novels: 'She writes about *my* feelings.'

In a secular world, Drabble's continuing spiritual anxieties have generally been overlooked. In *The Waterfall* and *The Needle's Eye* the heroines, Jane and Rose, suffer from religious neurosis, a conviction that they are damned and predestined to hell. This fear, which Drabble herself suffered in pubescence, derives from the Calvinistic Methodism of Drabble's forebears. When my book, *Margaret Drabble: Puritanism and Permissiveness*, the first full-length study of her work, appeared in 1974, she wrote: 'I am . . . grateful to you for pointing out that my books are not about feminism or babies, but salvation' (Letter, 26 October 1974). Her work is soaked with references to Bunyan[9] (the archetypal puritan, of whom Coleridge[10] wrote that never had Calvinism been painted in such soft colours), the Bible and the mystics. In *The Middle Ground* (1980), p. 224, she cites Meister Eckhard.[11] She is not sure whether God is there or not, but spiritual crisis is ever-present. How, asks Drabble, in a secular world where social justice seems as far away as ever, morality has decayed (in *The Garrick Year* the narrator mentions 'our tatty sexual decadence'), and we are threatened with new environmental problems, are we to find salvation? Her work offers an intelligent critique of society and an ongoing debate. The *New York Times Book Review* has opined that when the history of the twentieth century comes to be written, it is to her work that the curious will turn, to find out what life in Britain was like during the period.[12] Her work shows development from an enclosed, almost solipsistic, female world, to social anthropology, mythology and the historical roots of human sacrifice and social pathology.

NOTES

1. She was made a Commander of the British Empire, an honour conferred by the Queen.
2. A mark of the highest distinction, above first-class honours.
3. C. H. Rolph (ed.), *The Trial of Lady Chatterley: Regina v. Penguin Books Ltd.*, pp. 100–1.
4. Among novelists who have studied at Newnham are Hilary Bailey, A. S. Byatt, Elaine Feinstein, Sue Limb, Jessica Mann, and Iris Murdoch (graduate student).
5. A character in Dickens's novel, *Bleak House* (1852–53), who neglects her own children to work for the natives of Borriaboola-Gha, a fictitious place in Africa. In *The Millstone* Rosamund wonders whether her parents are not, in their own way, as cruel as Dr. Sloper in Henry James's novel, *Washington Square* (1881).
6. Frank Raymond Leavis (1895–1978). His revaluation, not just of the canon of English literature, but of the status of criticism, was profoundly influential in Cambridge until about 1980, when structuralism became the fashion. Leavis declared himself a 'puritan' and deeply admired Bunyan.
7. John Maynard Keynes (1883–1946) believed unemployment should be cured by government intervention. This view contrasted with classical economics, recently embraced once more by Mrs. Thatcher, who believes in *laissez-faire* and market forces.
8. British Council recorded interview with Valerie Grosvenor Myer (British Council, RI 2007, 1977).
9. John Bunyan (1628–88), author of a religious allegory, *The Pilgrim's Progress* (1678), until recently a standard part of the British junior

school curriculum. Bunyan was convinced he was in danger of hell-fire. He is one of Protestantism's heroes, who suffered imprisonment for his faith.
10. Samuel Taylor Coleridge (1772–1834), poet, critic and philosopher.
11. Johannes Eckhard (?1260–1327), father of German religious mysticism.
12. Phyllis Rose, *New York Times Book Review*, 7 September 1980, wrote: '. . . the chronicler of contemporary Britain, the novelist people will turn to in a hundred years from now to find out what things were like, the person who will have done for late twentieth-century London what Dickens did for Victorian London, what Balzac did for Paris.'

1

A Summer Birdcage (1963)

This novel went unsolicited to Weidenfeld and Nicolson, where it was rescued from 'the slush pile' (manuscripts which arrive unendorsed by literary agents), and Margaret Drabble, aged 24, was launched. It is a tale of two sisters called Bennett, inviting comparison with Jane Austen's *Pride and Prejudice*. It was crisp and amusing, contemporary: the narrator feels 'classlessness and social dislocation', having come down from Oxford with a first but no sense of vocation. Sarah sometimes feels the only benefit her education has bestowed is 'the ability to think in quotations'. The family background is not happy: the father, mentioned briefly, is a Birmingham businessman', a 'brute' and a 'reactionary'. The mother twitters. In a much anthologized scene, mother and daughter discuss Sarah's career. Trying not to be possessive, Sarah's mother says, 'I shall lose all my little ones at one fell swoop, shall I?' She's making a feeble joke, echoing Shakespeare's *Macbeth*, quoting Macduff's words when he learns his children have been murdered. Sarah's mother claims pity for her neglected self, while pathetically denying that she clings to her children. 'In my day, education was kept for the boys, you know.' Sarah replies, 'Well, you hadn't any boys to educate, had you? You had to make do with us.'

> And what thanks do I get. . . . I sometimes wonder what you and Louise bother to come home for. . . . You just use home as if it were a hotel. . . . All I am is a servant. . . . I know there's nothing to keep you here. . . . You always were too clever for me. . . .

Yet despite mama's sentimentality, the family is not truly affectionate: they shrink from touching one another (a recurrent motif in Drabble's work—maturity means the ability to hug and kiss).

Sarah's suburban home, comfortable but tasteless, with wall-lights like candles and chiming doorbell, stifles her; abroad has offered temporary escape. She plans to marry, but not yet. Sarah, like her friends in the novel, is nostalgic about Oxford, and her trip abroad has been an attempt to put off the everyday reality of Britain, 'this foul ugly country where people never smile at you or pinch your bottom'. She prefers Italy:

> Florence, Arno, Ferrara, Siena, Venice, Tintoretto, Cimabue, Orvieto, Lachrimae Christi, permesso, limonata . . . I am a nut case about abroad . . . I love E. M. Forster for loving it: I love George Eliot for her monstrous dedicated ardour in *Romola*: I love those two lines of Keats which I first found used to illustrate some long-forgotten figure of speech in a grammar textbook
> —So the two brothers and their murdered man
> Rode past fair Florence.[1]

A further submerged reference to Keats comes in the account of Kirstin, the Swedish *au pair*, who weeps into the washing up, 'depressed among the alien dishes.[2] I had been *au pair* myself.' Margaret Drabble was *au pair* in Paris and felt lost and lonely. In the novel, papa calls the girl a slut and mama 'launches into tirades of abstract liberal fervour'. When cousin Michael suggests Kirstin is sex-starved: ' "Oh, don't be stupid," I said, slipping back at once into my annoyed feminist we-are-as-frail-as-our-complexions—are mood.' Here the submerged allusion is to Shakespeare's *Measure for Measure*.[3]

On the train home, Sarah reads *Tender is the Night*, which she awards a 'beta minus'. She is en route to her sister's wedding, feeling that Louise is like Cinderella, while she is the ugly sister. When Louise condescends, carelessly, to be friendly, Sarah has to look at her experience through the lens of literature: it is 'like something out of *Middlemarch* or Jane Austen'. It is hard for us to take Louise at Sarah's valuation: she seems stuck up and rude. Sarah realizes that her sister's hostility was founded in jealousy.

> Until I went up to Oxford I always believed that the defensive, almost whining position that she invariably pushed me into

22

was the fault of my own miserable nature, as I admired her fanatically: it was only at university that I realised that it was she that forced me into grudgingness.

In an astonishing scene Louise gets drunk on the night before her wedding, spilling cigarette ash, her face shiny with cold cream. Despite being a knockout beauty, crazy about expensive clothes, Louise is a slut who gets married in a dirty bra, worn all the preceding week.

> 'I say, Sarah, what do you think it would feel like to be a virgin bride?'
> 'Terrifying, I should think . . . surely one would feel like a lamb led to the slaughter?'

At the wedding, Sarah recalls a bit of mildly bawdy bit of British folklore:

> As we waited for Louise, I remembered how she once told a whole railway compartment as we went through Chesterfield station that the tower leaned over because it saw a virgin bride.

The 'tower' is the spire of Chesterfield Church, actually twisted.

Louise is described by another character, Tony, as an 'ice-queen'. But her appearance of purity is as false as her feeling for Stephen Halifax, the man she marries, a rich, sneering novelist, a suppressed homosexual who lives off family money. He is apparently impotent with Louise, who before and after her mercenary marriage is having an affair with a vital, sexy actor, but marries Stephen for his money. Like Dorothea Casaubon in George Eliot's *Middlemarch* (1871), who is also married disastrously to a man we suspect is impotent, Louise on her honeymoon wanders disconsolately round Rome. The relationship is doomed.[4]

Eventually Sarah gains power over her sister and is, improbably, rewarded with Louise's affection. Louise is thrown out in her dressing-gown by Stephen after he finds her in the bath with John in Stephen's house, and Sarah is persuaded to take her in, though she has a potential lover of her own in her flat. This act of generosity to Louise, who is 'ungenerous', puts an end, we are asked to believe, to a 'basic antipathy . . .

23

long-rooted suspicion'. The sisters have briefly come together in the feminine pastime of showing clothes, but there is coldness between them. The mercenary marriage and the farcical dénouement are, of course, fictions, but the sibling rivalry is drawn from experience.[5] Marie Drabble, unprompted, offered me the information that the novel reflected the relations between Drabble and her elder sister, Antonia Susan. 'Susan' resented the birth of a second child, and 'Margaret was quite old before she realised that Susan didn't like her.' Marie added that reading Margaret's books embarrassed her: 'I said to her, "It's like reading your diary." ' While the temptation to read fiction as autobiography must be resisted, novelists invent events in order to write out their emotional experiences. While on the surface *A Summer Birdcage* is about the recovery of familial love, it is in fact a power struggle in which Sarah triumphs over the sister who 'always wins'. A. S. Byatt's response to *A Summer Birdcage* was her second novel, *The Game* (1967). Rivalry exists between an older sister who is a scholar and a young one who is a fashionable novelist (the family portrait is hardly fictionalized). The novelist humiliates her elder sister by mocking her in a novel, driving the victim to suicide.

At the end of *A Summer Birdcage* Louise seems to have perverted Sarah's moral values, or else the narrative holds lurking insincerity: on hearing that Louise married for money, Sarah is 'full of shock and *admiration*' (italics added). She says, 'I think it's rather a thrilling thing to do, to marry for money.' Louise corrects her: '. . . it's rather a cynical thing to do.' 'You're a right bitch, aren't you,' she says *admiringly* (italics added).

Louise does not seem to have learned from her disasters: 'Don't you ever marry for love, Sarah. It does terrible things to people.' Sarah does, however, reflect: 'So does the other thing.'

Louise cites another friend from Oxford, stuck in domestic squalor, with a husband who lectures at the Polytechnic, and they live in a 'slum' in Streatham with two unplanned babies, and poor Stella is on the verge of a nervous breakdown because her life is so awful.

The ending of *A Summer Birdcage* is no solution to Sarah's problem; Sarah is searching for love and for a place in the world. Her lover, Francis, at the end is 'somewhere across the Atlantic', which recalls the implied fate of Lucy Snowe's lover, Paul Emanuel, in Charlotte Brontë's *Villette* (1853): 'The Atlantic was strewn with wrecks.' As Kate Millett has demonstrated, Lucy is ambivalent about her lover,[6] and Sarah has deliberately encouraged hers to go away. As in Charlotte Brontë's *Shirley* (1849), Drabble's leading character—if we take Caroline Helstone and not the eponymous heroine to be the real subject—is at a loose end. Caroline's emotional crisis is healed by family love in the shape of a long-lost mother. Drabble herself says that when she started writing she was 'naïve': 'I thought all novels were about sisters.'[7] The novel has antecedents. In Rosamond Lehmann's distinguished *The Echoing Grove* (1957) sisters battle it out for the elder one's husband. After the death of Rollo the philanderer, Madeleine, the elder sister, reflects, 'We are both widows.' The sisters are reconciled, neither having won. Rosamond Lehmann, drawing on her experiences at Girton, also wrote the first novel about women at university, and the withdrawal symptoms on leaving Cambridge, in *Dusty Answer* (1927). Even more potent is E. Arnot Robertson's *Ordinary Families* (1933), in which the younger sister, Lalage, feels hopelessly inferior to the beautiful, promiscuous Margaret (who eventually steals Lalage's husband). *Ordinary Families* is a story of defeat.

Drabble's Sarah runs away from a party at Louise's elegant, but inhuman, married home 'as though chains had been loosened from my ankles, as though a burden had been lifted from my back'. We are reminded of Christian, in Bunyan's *The Pilgrim's Progress*, whose burden rolls off his back as he starts out on his journey. Yet she has nowhere much to run to. She tries flat-sharing with a college friend, Gill, whose marriage has failed. In the original version of the story, Gill's unhappy marriage was analysed, but editors pruned this section. The Gill scenario is promising, and the reader regrets the excision. Gill has grown tired of poverty and struggle and being taken for granted and, against her instincts, has had an abortion. She has left her husband, although she loved him, because she found life with him impossible. Gill's mother is 'a prison-visiting Quaker', who objects to her son-in-law's total lack of responsibility and social conscience, and his habitual promiscuity, of which she has somehow heard. Gill and Sarah finally get on each other's nerves, and Gill goes back to her parents. Gill's friends fail to impress Sarah, who casts a cold eye on their phoneyness, Bohemianism and dirt. Louise has disappeared. Sarah does not

> . . . think the drabness and despair which threatened to ooze over my life in every unoccupied second would ever swamp Louise: she was way off, wealthy, up in the sky and singing.

Sarah wonders why she 'couldn't . . . jump for the unreliable with both eyes shut, as Gill had done? Why did I want to have my cake and eat it. . . .' The lure of the unreliable, but sexy, male will recur in Drabble's novels. Gill refers to 'blighting the marriage hearse with a few odd tears'. The reference is to William Blake (1757–1827). The poem is 'London', from his *Songs of Experience* (1789–94). Drabble's characters talk easily in quotations. Sarah regrets not being so beautiful as Louise, but is thankful she is not ugly like their cousin Daphne, a spinster schoolmistress. Daphne 'makes me confess how much I am a bitch. And Daphne, who was chased by a god and was turned into a tree to preserve her virginity. . .'. The classical Daphne is put to subtler, more integrated use in *The Ice Age* (1977), as we shall see.

Another of Sarah's friends is the half-French, half-Italian Simone. She writes an affectionate, literary letter to Sarah, which delights her, though it strikes me as affected. It is impossible to say how far we may distance ourselves from young Sarah. Simone's writing is a 'black, twiglike script'; she has left Sarah a note with 'a black twig with one yellow flower like a Japanese painting'. Simone's aura strikes one as imagist, recalling petals on a wet black bough.

> Sad, eclectic gaunt Simone, with her dark face and her muddled heritage, her sexless passions and her ancient clothes, gathered from all the attics of Europe. . . . She moves through a strange impermanent world where objects are invested with as much power as people, and places possibly with more.

Simone represents the pure intellectuality of the French tradition, which does not provide all Sarah wants. The name Simone is no accident: Drabble had read Simone de Beauvoir's *The Second Sex* (first published in England 1953), and been profoundly disturbed by it. She has said she finds existentialism an inadequate view of life, but the intellectual, the academic, has its attractions. Embarking on a five-year stint as editor of *The Oxford Companion to English Literature*, published in 1985, she said, 'I love scholarship, I just love it.' She was taking up the option she had missed at 21. Simone's is

> . . . a wholly willed, a wholly undetermined life. And how could such a person love? The French believe they can, but one has only to read their books to mark some heroic disloca-tion from the pulse of continuous life. . . .

Heroic or not, dislocation will not do.

The problems of freedom and necessity, foreknowledge, will and fate, run through Drabble's fictions. In Gill, Sarah has seen 'the traditional university woman, badly dressed, censorious, and chaotic'. Sarah thought of staying on at uni-versity, but knows 'you can't be a sexy don.' The stereotype, like Daphne's, of the unattractive 'clever woman' was potent enough, in the 1960s, to frighten us all. Yet university educa-tion was then a rarer privilege than now, and brought with it obligations. Another school friend of Sarah's is a probation officer:

> . . . her moral streak had come out on top. . . . I didn't feel it was wholly my own love of luxury that was preventing me, either. . . . My moral streak was more ravenous and more demanding. I couldn't satisfy it with a sacrifice.

Sarah says: 'I'm not getting married. Catch me at the kitchen sink.' She takes a copy of *Paradise Lost* with her to read at a party, emblem of her university education and her nostalgia for it. Young Margaret Drabble, who had married immediately on graduating, explores in this novel the possibilities for educated women. The lineaments of Drabble woman, with whom a generation of readers easily identified, were set: literary, hungry, faintly attracted to the corrupt, torn between morality and desire. In her next novel, the narrator heroine shares some characteristics with Simone but, although clever, Emma is not educated.

27

The title of *A Summer Birdcage* comes from John Webster and is a comment on marriage:

> 'Tis just like a summer bird-cage in a garden: the birds that are without despair to get in, and the birds that are within despair and are in a consumption for fear they shall never get out.

Margaret Drabble's next heroine is stuck firmly in the marital cage, with two young children.

NOTES

1. John Keats (1795–1821). The lines are from a narrative poem, 'Isabella', Stanza XXVII. The figure of speech is prolepsis, or anticipation. The brothers, at this point, are *intending* to murder Isabella's lover, an intention later carried out.
2. Keats's 'Ode To a Nightingale': '. . . the sad heart of Ruth, when, sick for home,/ She stood in tears among the alien corn'. In the Bible (Book of Ruth), Ruth, a native of Moab, after being widowed follows her mother-in-law, Naomi, back to Judah. She is an emblem of loyalty and (since Keats) of homesickness. Ruth goes to work in the fields of Boaz, a wealthy relative of Naomi and eventually marries him.
3. In *Measure for Measure*, Act II, Sc. iii, Isabella says that women 'are soft as our complexions are/ And credulous to false prints'. The image is of wax, which takes it impression from a hard seal or stamp. Juan Luis Vives (1492–1540), cited by Hardin Craig in *The Enchanted Glass*, said the complexion (or temperament) of women was 'warm, soft and impressionable'. Craig adds that in Elizabethan psychology women were frail by nature and susceptible; they were strong in passion, weak in reason. Compare Shakespeare's 'The Rape of Lucrece', line 1240: 'For men have marble, women waxen minds', and *Twelfth Night*, Act II, Sc. ii: 'How easy is it for the proper false/ In women's waxen hearts to set their forms.' In Cyril Tourneur's *The Atheist's Tragedy* (1611), Act II, Sc. v, the lascivious Levidulcia says: 'Ladies are as courteous as yeomen's wives. . . . Hot diet and soft ease makes 'em (like wax always kept warm) more easy to take impression.' Sir Thomas Browne, in *Religio Medici* (1642), opposes marble to wax in a context of morality: 'I have no conscience of marble to resist the hammer of more heavy offences; nor yet so soft and waxen as to take the impression of each single pecadillo or scrape of infirmity.'
   Here, though, the 'frail-as-our-complexions-are' image is strangely applied: are we to believe that Sarah concurs with the view of

women's weakness? If, as she says, her mood is 'feminist', then this seems inconsistent.

4. The elaborate parallels between *Middlemarch* and *A Summer Birdcage* are amplified by Susanna Roxman in *Guilt and Glory* (pp. 14–18).

5. The issue is discussed in the British Council recorded interview with Valerie Grosvenor Myer. Drabble: 'Sisters are jealous of sisters.'

6. Kate Millett, *Sexual Politics* (Pt. 2, Ch. 4).

7. Myer interview.

2

The Garrick Year (1964)

Sarah, in *A Summer Birdcage* reflects:

> I don't know why I punish myself so. . . . I can't enjoy
> myself unless I do everything the hard way. Perhaps . . . the
> feeling of relief can only be savoured after undergoing the full
> initiation of effort.

This is the authentic note of Drabble woman: Emma Evans,
narrator–heroine of the second novel, tries to be a hedonist,
but is also strenuous. Daughter of a Cambridge theologian (a
transparent device which allows her to be nostalgic for Cambridge parties), Emma did not fulfil her father's expectation
that she would go to university, but instead became a fashion
model. She was sent away to an 'expensive and cranky girls'
school . . . in a country house with yellow stone and garden
statues'.

Then lucky Emma spends a year in Rome, 'just behind
the Piazza Navona', and two years in a flat in Primrose
Hill, which, 'though not of the classical and aristocratic
grandeur to which I was accustomed, had a visual cachet of
its own'.

As the story opens, Emma and David are living in Islington.
Drabble and her first husband lived in Islington, a district
then just rising into fashion. (Its humble place on the London
Monopoly board[1] is misleading: it is now a very expensive
area.) In the novel Emma cites

> . . . an old man who had lived in the house through all the
> permutations of the area from its days of respectable solidar-
> ity, the days in which Dickens refers to 'shady Pentonville',
> through the shabby slip into dusty urban poverty and back

once more into the classless rise of chi-chi that David and myself represented.

The old man, of course, could hardly have survived since Dickens's day—Charles Dickens, the novelist, died in 1870—but London districts go up and down in the social scale. In the 1960s it was a common delusion that social class had disappeared, though in fact the boundaries were merely re-aligning themselves. Actors and 'yuppies' (young upwardly mobile professionals, many of them actually in new semi-professions), models and photographers were the new rich, rising in prestige to challenge the traditional learned professions. Emma knows her 'tastes are shallow, my life is shallow'; she knows the glitterati 'do not count', but 'I depend'. She likes the flashy. Now she is married, resentfully, with two small children. Her problem is one which many women, particularly in the ensuing years, were to recognize: offered a job reading the news on television (at the time of writing, this was a fantasy, as women news-readers were unknown), she is dragged off to the provinces when her husband's career demands it. They move to the real town of Hereford, but to a fictional theatre. Emma outwardly acquiesces, but inwardly resists.

It is an open secret that the novel arose out of Drabble's boredom and resentment when she followed her husband to the Royal Shakespeare Theatre at Stratford-on-Avon, where he played good parts while she understudied, but the stars remained, in her own words, 'disgustingly healthy'. But Emma is not the serious, intellectual Miss Drabble; or if she is, Emma represents rebellion against circumstances by means of exploring a fictional alter ego, irresponsible, selfish and immature, like the child's imaginary companion who does all the 'naughty' things the child cannot admit to. Drabble herself says the novel probably contained much 'undigested unhappiness'.[2] When I first interviewed Drabble in 1970 for the *Times Educational Supplement*, I told her I read it as a satirical portrait of a silly woman, but Drabble retorted, 'She's not silly!' Drabble has respect for her character and sympathy with Emma's plight (which was in many respects her own). I then assumed she was on the side of Emma's old school-friend, Mary Scott, the calm, correct, uncreative and rather dull school-friend who has always mistrusted Emma's 'vein of perversity', from a professional background. Mary's father is a solicitor. Mary is in schematic opposition to the actress Sophy Brent, who is beautiful, 'ripe', 'like fruit', elegant, sexy, but untalented and remarkably stupid. 'But Sophy has so much more openness to life', said Drabble. Yet I feel, even now, that in this endorsement there is something willed, factitious; in the Drabble *oeuvre* there is an ongoing conflict between the natural and the civilized and, much as Drabble might wish to find the natural, it is a struggle for her, as author, to shrug off the moralistic inheritance. The American scholar Ellen Cronan Rose has written a study of Drabble with the title, *Equivocal Figures: The Novels of Margaret Drabble*[3], exploring ambiguity; and the Canadian scholar Nora Foster Stovel has analysed Drabble's patterns of imagery in a distinguished book entitled *Margaret Drabble: Symbolic Moralist*.[4] Mary and Sophy are a schematic contrast as were Gill and Simone in the previous novel. Emma is competitive: she would rather have Sophy's dislike (implying respect) than her affection. She is humiliated when she discovers that Sophy is David's mistress.

This second book was serialized on B.B.C. 'Woman's Hour' and made Drabble famous. It has the virtues of its predecessor: alert observation, wit, a fast-moving story. Emma (a name which recalls Jane Austen's Emma Woodhouse who learns from experience, and Flaubert's Emma Bovary who commits adultery and dies) commits adultery and lives. But it is a very strange adultery, consisting of endless dinners out and rides in cars, and caresses restricted to above the waist. Emma declares a 'passion' for her lover, but it is more like a schoolgirl crush; the affair is consummated only once, briefly, when she is in bed with a cold, and she does not enjoy it. Emma does not seem to like sex much at all: she describes herself as 'frigid' and tells her husband the children were the result of 'legalised rape'. Her husband seems even more selfish than she is. However, Emma has chosen him with the perversity which is an admitted aspect of her character: she is excited by domination and threat, though she sulks at the practical effects. She strikes martyred attitudes. She has

imagined married life would be a 'nightmare, an adventure
. . . whatever else exciting . . . I did not want an easy life, I
wanted something precipitous.' She enjoys his violence and
is full of *admiration* (italics added) when he thumps a wall,
shattering plaster and tearing a hole in expensive William
Morris wallpaper. Emma is attracted by David's 'flashy,
commercial, drunken, photogenic selfishness' and he by
her 'cool professional aesthetic privileged photogenic eccen-
tricity'. Emma is beautiful in a bony, stick-like, dun-coloured
way and has appeared on the covers of glossy magazines. It
is hardly surprising that so many readers choose to identify
with Drabble woman, who is always good-looking, always
intelligent and usually at some point of female crisis.

Passion, in the Evans ménage, is soon 'choked by domesticity': the couple have 'married in haste and repented at
leisure'. As in the previous book, there are many journeys by
public transport, but in those days, as the author comments,
few actors had cars. 'Our affluence, like that of so many
actors, went hand in hand with a disastrous lack of capital.'
His extravagance is what attracted her to him, but 'compared
to him, I am as mean as hell. . . . I am always trying to do
without, just to practise, just in case, and this annoys him.'

Emma's legs are badly crushed (but heal) after an accident
with her lover's car, and she finds her true self when she
rescues her daughter from drowning in the river Wye. This
plot cliché is a symbolic baptism, as I have pointed out in
a previous study.[5] Childfree Sophy, dropping by in pursuit
of David, finds Emma 'fishing boiling hot nappies out of
the washing machine with a pair of wooden tongs'. Until
about 1980, disposable nappies (diapers) were unknown,
and towelling nappies were rinsed and washed. Emma has a
washing machine, but no spin-dryer; she relies on a mangle
to extract surplus water. For many women readers, this story
with its background of breast-feeding, nappy-washing and
the struggle for identity when swamped in domesticity is
the archetypal Drabble story, and remains a favourite. Just
as its predecessor offers a wish-fulfilment victory to jealous
younger sisters, so Emma, despite being 'rotten with grief',
offers vicarious glamour; she may feel trapped, but she lives
among actors, she is elegant, she manages to find a lover,

even though she does not actually like him or his company all that much, and suspects (rightly) that the wretched man hopes she will sew a button on for him. With him she has found a limited escape, a temporary freedom (she has an *au pair* to leave the children with, and her husband works in the evenings). At the end of the season, the lover moves on, causing her only, it seems, physical pain. That she is reconciled to her husband at the end seems arbitrary; the dénouement is not what one remembers. One remembers Emma's frustration and hunger for recognition and excitement, not her come-uppance, or the tears of repentance she weeps over Wordsworth, the touchstone, for Drabble, of truth.

NOTES

1. Monopoly is a board game in which the players buy houses and hotels, the value of the property depending on the value of the district.
2. British Council interview with Valerie Grosvenor Myer.
3. Ellen Cronan Rose, *Equivocal Figures: The Novels of Margaret Drabble* (London: Macmillan, 1980).
4. Nora Foster Stovel, *Margaret Drabble: Symbolic Moralist* (Mercer Island: Starmont House, 1989). I have deposited most of my Drabbleana with Dr. Stovel for her archive. Newnham were not interested.
5. Valerie Grosvenor Myer, *Margaret Drabble: Puritanism and Permissiveness* (London: Vision Press; New York: Barnes & Noble, 1974).

3

The Millstone (1965)

Sarah, in *A Summer Birdcage*, Drabble's first heroine/narrator, was worried about privilege, although she hungered for 'luxury'. The novel ends (though it is not resolved) by her drawing closer to her sister. Aristocratic Emma in *The Garrick Year* is saved from self-absorption by the rescue of her daughter from drowning. Drabble justifies this cliché by saying that when she was at Stratford-on-Avon, two people actually were drowned. With Rosamund Stacey, first-person narrator of *The Millstone*, in a subtle and multi-layered novel, one of Drabble's themes is an enquiry into the nature of socialism as practised by the upper middle class. Rosamund discovers community by giving birth.

Rosamund has resented her parents' self-sacrificing principles and habits of self-punishment, but has imbibed their values. They are well-known socialist academics, offstage during the action of the novel. Their 'over-healthy' attitude to sex has left her terrified of it, terrified of human contact other than the superficial and social, abnormally reticent and polite. Rosamund, telling her story, reveals in another memorable comic scene how she intended to spend the night with a young man in a hotel, but carelessly signed the register with her own name. Grudgingly, they were allowed into the hotel (the novel appeared in 1965, when couples sharing hotel rooms pretended, at least, to be married). Yet although the receptionist 'gave us our key', Rosamund remains a virgin.

A literary lady, Rosamund thinks she ought to carry a scarlet letter A on her bosom, not for Adultery, like the American writer Nathaniel Hawthorne's Hester Prynne, in his novel

The Scarlet Letter (1850), but for Abstinence: in our era a sin, as Rosamund wryly reflects. Rosamund thinks, like Sarah, in quotations; researching into Elizabethan sonnet sequences, she mentions Samuel Daniel, author of a poem called 'The complaint of Rosamond', Michael Drayton, George Herbert, Sir Walter Raleigh, Ben Jonson (all Elizabethan/Jacobean poets), the allegorist John Bunyan, the novelist Thomas Hardy's *Tess of the D'Urbervilles* and *Life's Little Ironies*, the critic Rosamund Tuve, who has analysed the images used by poets of the Renaissance, the medieval Scottish poet Robert Henryson, the French philosopher Voltaire, the English novelist and journalist Daniel Defoe, the Greek philosophers Plato and Aristotle and their conflicting theories of literature, Richmal Crompton (1890–1969), author of the popular 'William' books, films directed by the Italian Federico Fellini and the Swedish Ingmar Bergman. Rosamund has the usual cosmopolitan culture of the Cambridge graduate. She employs a cleaning lady called Mrs. Jennings, who is fat: Mrs. Jennings is the name of the vulgar, but kindly, mother of Lady Middleton in Jane Austen's novel, *Sense and Sensibility* (1811). Jane Austen's Mrs. Jennings is also fat, so we know that Rosamund's Mrs. Jennings, too, will be all right, even if she does belong to the charwoman class. Rosamund's own name has associations: Fair Rosamond, mistress of King Henry II of England, lived secluded in the middle of a labyrinth at Woodstock. Rosamund Stacey (and it has been suggested that her name is suggestive of *stasis*) is in the metaphorical 'ivory tower' of scholarship. Living rent-free in the empty flat of her parents, who are away doing unspecified good works in Africa, she is multiply privileged. She is confident that her education has equipped her to earn a living. (In the 1960s, Britain had full employment, and certainly no unemployed Ph.Ds.) Rosamund has two writer friends, Joe (who writes bad, successful novels) and Lydia (who seems to write good, but unsuccessful, ones, though this is only hinted). Both these writers come from the poorer classes and have known hardship. Lydia, moving into Rosamund's flat, says: 'It's so *posh* round here, and you're so posh, and I do have such a thing about being posh.'

Going about with her platonic boyfriend Roger the barrister, Rosamund is embarrassed by his High Tory arrogance and chauvinism. She oscillates between him and Joe, the novelist who has risen from poverty, as escorts. Each is convinced she is sleeping with the other, a convenient evasion. She is unaligned politically, as she is sexually, until the single encounter which leaves her pregnant. But she does some teaching, to make money and because of her 'social conscience'. Rosamund's pregnancy (she is unmarried) draws her into National Health hospitals and astonished contact with the working classes. She is not rich, but she is comfortably placed. Despite her theoretically liberal political stance, the reality of deprivation in others comes as a shock: 'The people that I was used to seeing on my home ground were a mixed enough lot, apart from the occasional freak, beggar or road worker. . . .' Now she notices a West Indian, a Pakistani, two Greeks, respectably shabby old people, and an old woman whose clothes are held together by safety pins, revealing layers of 'fraying, loose-stitched, hand-knitted cardigans in shades of maroon, dark blue and khaki'. The woman's legs 'overflow' her ankles. Rosamund wonders where the well-dressed people are, and concludes they must be in Harley Street (which she cannot afford). Rosamund's own complaints seem 'so trivial in comparison with the ills of age and worry and penury' that she wonders whether it is worth bothering the doctor at all to tell him she is pregnant. The sentence echoes Shakespeare's *Measure for Measure*, Act 3, Sc. i:

> The weariest and most loathéd worldly life
> That age, ache, penury and imprisonment
> Can lay on nature—is a paradise
> To what we fear of death.

Rosamund's first experience of a maternity clinic comes as a shock; she does not expect to have to wait, but soon becomes adept at slipping her card into the pile so as to be called earlier. It is a shock to be internally examined by five medical students, one after another. Eventually she is drawn into the conversation with the other pregnant women, despite being 'trebly outcast by my unmarried status, my education, and my class'. At the end of six months' attendance, the 'pull of nature' is so strong that 'I felt more in common with the ladies of the clinic than with my own acquaintances.' 'The pull of nature' recalls Shakespeare once again: 'One touch of nature makes the whole world kin' (*Troilus and Cressida*, Act III, Sc. iii).

Rosamund now discovers that the fresh facts which break in on her consciousness are the ones her 'admirable parents had always so firmly presented . . . inequality, . . . limitation, . . . separation, . . . the impossible, heart-breaking uneven hardship of the human lot'. Rosamund has always felt for others in theory, but now, pregnant, she feels in the heart. 'Hitherto in my life I had most successfully avoided the bond that links man to man, though I had paid it some lip service.' She has considered it immoral to 'pay anyone to do dirty work that I could do myself'. This attitude is the result of her upbringing, though she knows it is 'not technically good socialism' and even her parents are not so scrupulous.

> It is not virtue, it is not morality: by my scruples I was denying some woman four bob[1] an hour for as many hours as it would have taken to rescue that large flat from the squalor into which it was forever threatening to sink. With a baby, though, I could not afford such scruples.

Rosamund is finally decided to employ help by the fact that babies cannot be taken into libraries, where she works.

There is considerable satire on the figure of Rosamund's sister Beatrice, a socialist who does not allow her children to play with the local kids because they use words like 'Silly bugger'. (Drabble was later distressed to find that this had been misread as a statement of endorsement, implying that indeed it is impossible to let well brought up children play with rough ones. She uses the National Health Service herself, and her children went to good state schools.) Beatrice's children are called Nicholas and Alexandra, the names of the last Emperor and Empress of Russia, murdered in 1917. The common little girl is called Sandra, a diminutive of Alexandra, showing she is a sister under the skin. Beatrice and Rosamund have been accused, by some boys in the park with whom they have innocently played, of being 'rich', when they mention they have a maid. Drabble, ever alert to social nuance, writes, in the persona of Rosamund, that although one is now (in the 1960s) uncomfortable about saying 'maid', it had been permissible a decade or so earlier. Beatrice's mind is 'preyed on' by the question of pacifism; although the parents in the novel are not Quakers (indeed, they seem to be agnostics), they are recognizably of the same breed as Gill's mother in *A Summer Birdcage*, the 'prison-visiting Quaker'. They also have points in common with Robin and Priscilla in Angus Wilson's short story, 'Such Darling Dodos'. Angus Wilson is a writer Drabble admires (he is one of those mentioned in *A Summer Birdcage*, along with Dr. Leavis, as among people who have done 'real things').[2] Poor Beatrice, unluckily for a pacifist, is married to a nuclear scientist. Beatrice reinforces Rosamund's isolation by advising her to have the baby adopted. Rosamund's sister-in-law, Clare, is no help: she gives dinner parties, endlessly visits the dry cleaners and the hairdresser (which Rosamund despises as a waste of time and money). Rosamund's brother, Andrew, has married a conventional member of their class. Rosamund reflects, with unconscious bitchiness, that she and her sister, and even their mother, are prettier than 'poor Clare', as well as being 'brighter'.

> But Oh God, I thought . . . whose fault is that, whose virtue, and my dislike ebbed away . . . leaving me . . . on the hard damp shore of sociological pity. Riches are a dreadful blight, and poor Clare hadn't even got riches: all she had was gentility and inherited voice.

It is not clear whether there is suppressed envy here on Rosamund's part; indeed, she seems remarkably free from envy, as she is moderately self-satisfied. She recognizes that life is not fair, and 'those who, like my parents, attempt to level it out are doomed to failure'. This insight of Rosamund's has led to arguments over the family breakfast table, when she was told that although nothing could be done about inequality of brains and beauty, perhaps it was worth doing something about economics. Poor Rosamund has been sent to 'a very good grammar school', where she was the only child of Labour-voting parents, although they were 'the poshest and most well-known'. Rosamund has been confused by this 'upside down' position.

Staying in hospital for ten days (then usual) after the birth of her baby, Rosamund is astonished at the conversation of ordinary, uneducated women. At that time, washing machines were a rare luxury, as were cars. Two women are discussing the comparative merits of the launderette and hand-washing at home. This comic dialogue, in which the women totally misunderstand each other, so that although they hold opposing views, each imagines she commands the support of the other, is richly comic. (It may have been as a result of this passage that Drabble was invited to advertise washing powder on television, an invitation she refused.) Other women in hospital talk about whether or not their families will, or will not, eat spinach.

Rosamund realizes that she would never have dared to have an illegitimate baby if she had not had a good social position, a good address:

> So . . . I was cashing in on the foibles of a society which I have always distrusted; by pretending to be above its strictures, I was merely turning its anomalies to my own use. *I would not recommend my course of action to anyone with a shade less advantage in the world than myself.* (italics added)

Octavia develops a heart defect. I imagined that the source must be literary and asked Drabble whether it came from Helen Thomas's *As It Was,* an account of her married life with the poet Edward Thomas (1878–1917): Helen's baby had a heart defect. But Drabble replied that she had never read Helen Thomas, and that one of her own babies had had heart trouble. Rosamund is not allowed to visit her baby in hospital, as was the fashion then: nurses said it 'unsettled' babies to see their mothers. Rosamund insists and finally screams and screams until the authorities give way, overruled by the surgeon, Dick Protheroe. Rosamund is 'pulling rank' on the nurses (whose conversation is depicted as pretty brainless) here, as the surgeon is an old friend of her father's.

The *Times Literary Supplement* review of *The Millstone* began:

The form of Margaret Drabble's cool and lucid novels is becoming familiar. She takes a clever, classy, arty but essentially self-contained modern girl and treats us to an exposition of her very reasoned and ordered inward musings. . . .

This seems fairly clear and simple: Drabble woman is now a recognizable type with minor variations, the first-person narrations inviting identification with the author, who is known herself to be privileged and good-looking and to share, to some extent, the problems of her narrators. The books all show humour, even wit: but are we meant to take Sarah, Emma and Rosamund at their own valuations? Is the joke ever at their expense? Lucidity may be deceptive. Drabble makes her characters contradict themselves, even lie to themselves. Whose voice is speaking, the character's or the author's? The fascinated readers who identify with Drabble woman are comparing themselves, if we look closely, to some very odd fish. Drabble's defence of these early *personae* (for example, her insistence in conversation with me that Emma in *The Garrick Year* is not silly and that Rosamund is young—'only 21!'), suggest she has felt the characters, at the time of writing at least, to be extensions of herself. Rosamund gets her doctorate the same year as she bears her illegitimate daughter Octavia, so she is more probably about 24. But Drabble was 21 when her first child was born.

The point may seem trivial, but as Susan Spitzer has pointed out in a stimulating essay, 'Fantasy and Femaleness in Margaret Drabble's *The Millstone*,[3] the tale contains ambiguities of which Rosamund is certainly unaware.

'To what extent', writes Spitzer, 'Margaret Drabble has expressed Rosamund's unconscious *unconsciously* it is difficult to say. . .'(88). Rosamund, however, goes to the doctor early in her pregnancy, driven by the 'fear of being made a fool of by my subconscious': she thinks her symptoms might be psychosomatic. Drabble herself, in an author's introduction to a school edition, sees Rosamund as telling her story 'with irony but without bitterness'.[4] Rosamund, for Drabble, is simply 'a lonely, proud and isolated person. . . . I wrote it while I was expecting my third baby. . . . In some ways I wrote . . . to cheer myself up . . . and trying to resolve the problem of why something that is so disagreeable and humiliating and at times painful and frightening should also be so important and rewarding' (vii). She considers Rosamund's single state unimportant and declares she wanted to write about the experience of maternity, 'the amazing delight I felt in my first baby'. Drabble considers that Rosamund treats George badly, in not letting him know the child is his: 'George would have been delighted to have both her and the child, had she given the smallest sign of wanting him' (xi).

But George seems to be bisexual, so he might not have been such a good bet after all. Drabble was alarmed to find that schoolgirls understood the book as encouragement to go and have babies while unmarried; she has been at pains to point out that Rosamund is privileged, has the use of her parents' flat and enough money to pay a minder while she gets on with her research, going every day to the British Museum library.

Spitzer remains uneasy:

> The few instances we may wish to take as distancing effects hardly cancel out our feeling that Rosamund is largely approved of and abetted by her author. . . . brief flickerings of illumination are rapidly snuffed out by cold gusts of fear habitually disguised as reason. . . . she, Rosamund, will be a good mother to *herself* through the intermediary of this child. . . .

That the Stacey parents are accused by Rosamund herself of distant coldness, a characteristic she has inherited, we know.

Spitzer is particularly good on Rosamund's real desire to give birth to the child, though Rosamund denies it by attempting to induce an abortion with gin and a hot bath, but friends drop by and drink the gin (another of Drabble's wryly memorable scenes). 'A failed attempt that was *meant* to fail: she almost realizes this, but not quite. . . . Yet it is clear', writes Spitzer, 'the abortion was never meant to succeed or else why couldn't she have begun the same procedure, or another, on the following day?'

To be fair, I believe Rosamund (and her creator) are perfectly well aware of this. Rosamund, like many women, both desires and fears motherhood. The ambivalence towards the parents is not in doubt, either. But where Spitzer's argument is unsettling is in her comment that Rosamund's dread of becoming like the poor women at the antenatal clinic betrays disgust:

> Anaemia and exhaustion were written on most countenances: the clothes were dreadful, the legs swollen, the bodies heavy and unbalanced. There were a few cases of striking wear: a huge middle-aged woman who could walk only with a stick, a pale thin creature with varicose veins and a two-year old child in tow, and a black woman who sat there not with the peasant acceptance of physical life of which one hears, but with a look of wide-eyed dilating terror.

(Spitzer does not comment on that surprising use of the gynaecologically suggestive word, 'dilating'.) Spitzer considers bodies repel Rosamund, reminding Rosamund of sex (which she has feared and avoided): all Rosamund's efforts, says Spitzer, 'continue to be made in the direction of denying her adult female body'.

In the novel, the act of birth, says Spitzer, has been 'downright *sterilised*', so easily does Rosamund have her child. In Spitzer's view, Rosamund's expression that the streets were 'crawling' with women invites the comparison with insects. Rosamund's flatmate Lydia looks 'dirty'.

> Lydia compares herself to a 'dirty great spider' dragging novels out of herself, while Rosamund 'does a job'. . . . the different modes of productivity [characterise] the 'female' Lydia and 'male' Rosamund; the novelist, subjective, attentive to the unconscious, the thesis-writer largely ignoring it, dealing with 'objective' reality.

Lydia is the splitting off of Rosamund's psyche, as Spitzer says, but the author knows that; Lydia the novelist, voracious for material, does not spin her webs totally out of herself—she engages with lived experience, and puts Rosamund into a novel. It is Lydia who reproaches Rosamund for her detachment. Again, all this is quite clear within the terms of the novel, which, like Shakespeare's plays within the play, challenges our notions of truth: *The Millstone* deals with the old problem of appearance and reality. It is Lydia who makes common-sense suggestions about the baby to Rosamund. When Octavia chews up the novel Lydia has written about Rosamund and Octavia, Rosamund thinks in literary parallels: she compares the incident to the accidental burning of the manuscript of Thomas Carlyle's *The French Revolution*. Lydia, in her distress at the destruction of her typewritten novel, of which there is no duplicate copy, is said to 'blench'. This is in fact an error for 'blanch', to turn white (the actual meaning of 'blench' is 'to turn aside'). Life, here, triumphs over art, though Rosamund's satisfaction in her baby's unconscious revenge shows a mean streak.

Spitzer believes that Rosamund's wit, along with the 'quasi-critical eye with which she regards herself', tends to seduce us into approving her and identifying with her. We do, but the corrective vision is also implied. Spitzer feels that *The Millstone* is a wish-fulfilling fantasy, in that Rosamund's knowledge is cheaply bought. Spitzer believes a baby girl will be 'a substitute penis'; her argument seems to be that Rosamund really want to be a man. The fulfilment of her womanhood in childbirth will be interpreted by her as a validating achievement which will make her adult. Remedying a 'primal hurt' when her mother preferred the father to the baby Rosamund, Rosamund rejects the 'bad penis', the penetrator: 'the body, as such, is repulsive and dangerous; she will therefore pretend it does not exist and take refuge in the mind, in reason, logic, "masculine" modes of perception. . . . The baby in this way can be seen to fulfil the traditional Freudian function of penis-substitute for the woman.'

To accept Spitzer's argument one has to go along with Freud's discredited concept of 'penis-envy'. But the reading of Rosamund and the conclusion that Margaret Drabble 'has an intuitive grasp of the workings of the unconscious' cannot easily be dismissed. There is no reason why they should be; however closely Drabble may identify her younger self with Rosamund, the alert reader does not. Drabble has described herself as 'a great Freudian' and was actually reading Freud when she wrote *The Millstone*. Rosamund herself, in the first chapter, admits to 'some deeply rooted Freudian reason' for writing her own name in the hotel register. Rosamund writes about her early experience with the reflective wisdom of comparative maturity.

Susanna Roxman dismisses Spitzer's essay as 'almost parodically Freudian',[5] and points out, rightly, that Lydia is 'grey' and looks dirty not because femaleness is disgusting but because as a child she had only bad food. Roxman does not comment, however, that Drabble gives to Lydia a 'dirty' expensive Aquascutum mackintosh, together with nervous tics like nail-chewing and eye-twitching. Rosamund is not over-fastidious herself, until she has the baby, when she becomes anxious about hygiene.

Just as in *The Garrick Year* characters discussed the theatre and its relation to reality, Rosamund and her friends discuss the art of fiction. Lydia is established at the start as having integrity: she says she could never do a book she knew was bad just to make money, but she admires those who can, because of the effort involved.

Lydia has been underprivileged before publishing a novel and has left school at 16. When *The Millstone* was filmed, under the title *A Touch of Love*, the rôle was played by Eleanor Bron, who, like Rosamund and Drabble herself, is a Cambridge graduate, physically fit and from a comfortable background. She would have been better cast as Rosamund, who for mysterious reasons was played, well, by an American actress, Sandy Dennis. Miss Dennis managed a good British accent and a convincing characterization, but Drabble's fictions do not dramatize well, because one does not read Drabble for her plots, but for complicity (as with Jane Austen) with the dazzlingly intelligent authorial voice. In America the novel was published under a different title again, *Thank You All Very Much*.

Roxman does not elaborate on the symbolic importance of Lydia's rôle. For Roxman the fact that Rosamund's parents work in India and Africa is 'the first hint in Drabble of a global approach to the problem of privilege', a valid point. 'There is considerable, but seldom recognized, irony in Drabble's novels', she adds. Drabble has frequently said how she admires Jane Austen, although she thinks George Eliot a greater writer. Drabble's pages are also haunted by the ghost of Henry James, who wrote in his novel, *The Aspern Papers* (1888): 'The historian, essentially, wants more documents than he can really use; the dramatist only wants more liberties than he can really take.' This dichotomy is imaged by Rosamund (who, like Emma, prefers facts to fiction) and Lydia the artist. The truths that Rosamund cannot see are subtly exemplified in Lydia's perceptions. For fuller discussion, see my earlier book and Nora Foster Stovel's. Stovel points out:

> Rosamund's reference to correcting 'the proofs of an article of mine on an article on a book on Spenser and Courtly Love' . . . makes it clear that her critical approach to her subject is particularly artificial, being at several removes from the real thing.[6]

'The real thing' is aptly used here, as it is a recurrent phrase in Drabble's work, and the title of story (also about art and life) by Henry James. Drabble, according to one commentator, wrote *The Millstone* in the British Museum Library, contained in its artificial womb, pregnant with her own baby, and giving symbolic birth to Rosamund's story, which is reflected within the novel by Lydia's version of it: experience at third remove.

This is all very elegant, but it is not true.[7] I checked with Drabble, who wrote (23 July 1990):

> I don't think I wrote The Millstone in the British Museum. Did I say I did somewhere? I wrote it in Riversdale Road, Highbury. I always type my novels so can't have written it in the BM though I may well have composed some of it there—I used to use the Reading Room on the odd day. . . . But mostly I worked at home.

Perhaps for this reason we do not altogether believe in Rosamund as a research student: she never seems to have to see a supervisor, for example. Rosamund, like subsequent heroines, whatever their nominal occupations, lives the life of the freelance writer, unconstrained by the organizational structures of postgraduate life, or its normal contacts. She does have a 'director of studies', like an undergraduate, who is a 'Cambridge don'. It is never explained why Rosamund is not doing research at Cambridge, where she went to university. Cambridge Ph.D. students are required to reside in Cambridge most of the time, and this detail is fudged. On getting married, Drabble left Cambridge to live in London, and does not bother to explain her heroine's circumstances. Rosamund represents for her barrister friend Roger, 'a raffish seedy literary milieu', to which she improbably belongs.

Rosamund is attracted to one man because he is so ugly and to George because she thinks he is gay. Rosamund, like Emma Evans, admits to being 'perverse', as indeed she is. Like Emma, who has an erotic dream about the homosexual Julian, Rosamund is attracted by the ambiguous George. It does not occur to her that her invitation to go up to her flat for coffee might be construed as a sexual invitation. She wants George 'in my bed all night, asleep on my pillow', but she can hardly admit her desire to herself, let alone to him. Going over the encounter in her mind, she decides it was all her fault for going to sit next to him on the settee: 'I had offered myself' and indeed she has. George does not telephone, though she expects him to: if, as Drabble says, George would have been happy to know about Octavia, why is he so uninterested in, almost passive in relation to, Octavia's mother? Drabble men tend to share her own passion for babies, but George's behaviour is as peculiar as Rosamund's. She declares she loves him, but nullifies his paternity.

Rosamund is perfectly aware of her own tendency to self-deception: she finds herself pretending she has to go shopping near Oxford Circus, near the B.B.C. where George works: 'I only just caught myself out in time.'

Drabble's own comment is,

> I think I was conscious in my early novels of the fact that the men were shadowy characters. This was partly through a reluctance on my part to blame men, which I still feel. I think that it's not proper to blame people for the bad situations in which women themselves have put their men. Certainly Rosamund in *The Millstone* is guilty of putting George in a very false situation. She behaves much worse than he does. He is vague only in that she can't see him clearly.[8]

The Millstone retains its popularity after a quarter of a century, because of its wit and its ambiguous truths. It has been much translated and studied abroad, partly because its language is comparatively simple. But its ironies, as Spitzer recognizes, are complex; *The Millstone* is a small masterpiece.

NOTES

1. 20 pence.
2. Drabble is currently at work on a biography of Angus Wilson.
3. Susan Spitzer, 'Fantasy and Femaleness in Margaret Drabble's *The Millstone*', *Novel*, 11, No. 3 (Spring 1978), 227–46. Reprinted in Ellen Cronan Rose (ed.), *Critical Essays on Margaret Drabble*, pp. 87–105.
4. Margaret Drabble, *The Millstone*, Longman Imprint edition, (London, 1979), p. viii.
5. Susanna Roxman, *Guilt and Glory*, p. 67.
6. Nora Foster Stovel, *Margaret Drabble: Symbolic Moralist*, p. 63.
7. Michael F. Harper points out that there are two versions of the genesis of *A Summer Birdcage*: that she started writing in the theatre dressing room, and that she began it when she found herself housebound with her first baby. Harper, 'Margaret Drabble and the Resurrection of the English Novel', *Contemporary Literature*, 23, No. 2 (Spring 1982), 145–68. Reprinted in Ellen Cronan Rose (ed.), *Critical Essays*, p. 52.
8. Interview with Diana Cooper Clark, *Atlantic Monthly*, 246, No. 5 (November 1980), 69–75. Reprinted in Rose (ed.), *Critical Essays*, p. 21.

4

Jerusalem the Golden (1967)

The story of Clara Maugham, born into the northern lower middle class, marks various new departures. This is Margaret Drabble's first novel to use (omniscient) third-person narration, and to move outside the world of comfort and privilege. Clara has been described by critics as 'cool', like the other girls, but by no means can she be described as 'classy'. She grows up in the fictional town of Northam (Sheffield? The Five Towns?), a suggestive name, which was in fact the name of a lecturer at Cambridge University when Drabble was at Newnham in the 1950s and where I followed her in 1963. Clara is intelligent, but a victim of a mean and stultifying background. The educational ladder is her escape, but that escape, as we shall see, is rife with ambiguities.

All three of Drabble's previous heroines move from self-centredness into relationship with other people: Clara has to find herself a substitute family, and in the Denhams she finds both a surrogate sister in Clelia and a lover in Clelia's married brother Gabriel. The family name is Denham, which has literary associations: Virginia Woolf's novel, *Night and Day* (1919), has a Ralph Denham, and Jane Austen's unfinished novel, *Sanditon*, has a Lady Denham, formerly 'a rich Miss Brereton, born to wealth, but not to education'. (In 1974, Drabble edited Jane Austen's *Lady Susan, The Watsons* and *Sanditon* for Penguin Books.) *Jerusalem the Golden* is full of explicit literary echoes.[1] Clara is like the children Cathy and Heathcliff in Emily Brontë's novel, *Wuthering Heights* (1847), when they peer through the windows of Thrushcross Grange, the outsider looking in. When Clara approaches the Denham house, built in 1720, her arrival parodies the scenes where the picaresque hero or heroine arrives at the Gothic mansion, notably in Charlotte Brontë's novel *Jane Eyre* (1847). Clara's own home is in Hartley Road, Northam. David Hartley (1705–1757) is remembered chiefly for his doctrines of 'association of ideas' and the 'vibrations'; Hartley believed that sensation was caused by a vibration of the minute particles of the medullary substance of the nerves made possible by the 'subtle elastic ether' postulated by the mathematician Sir Isaac Newton (1642–1727). The poet Samuel Taylor Coleridge was for a while an enthusiast for Hartley's opinions, and named his first son Hartley, before deciding that he preferred synthesis to analysis. Coleridge came to reject David Hartley's doctrine of vibrations as mechanistic. By the end of the eighteenth century, Newton's world-view was under attack. The poets William Blake (1757–1827) and John Keats (1795–1821) specifically attacked Newton in their poetry.[2] In Charlotte Brontë's novel *Shirley*, Michael Hartley is a crazed, Antinomian weaver: a man whose dependence on reason has led him to lose all sense of right and wrong. Hartley's name is identified with psychological materialism, opposed to Romantic vitalism. Drabble is the admirer of, and author of a book on, the Romantic poet William Wordsworth (1770–1850), and has described his autobiographical poem, 'The Prelude', about 'the growth of a poet's mind', as 'a great psychological novel'.[3] Typically of English writers, especially those who have been through the Cambridge school of English literature, she generally follows the trend of English novelists from the Romantics through Dickens to E. M. Forster in taking the Romantic, as opposed to the Utilitarian, view of life, with a belief in the organic.

In *Jerusalem the Golden*, structure and plot recall not only William Makepeace Thackeray's novel *Vanity Fair* (1847), as has been frequently noted, but also Honoré de Balzac's novel, *Père Goriot* (1834), where the young provincial Rastignac makes his way into society and discovers its corruption. (Drabble knows and speaks French well, and has made translations of, for example, Sartre, though she finds 'the existentialist writers very arid'.[4]) Clara, on her first visit to Paris, wanders round Montmartre on her own, rather as Daisy Miller in Henry James's story of that name does Rome, but without fatal results. Drabble has remarked:

> The writers that I most admire are the people who strive to retain their links with the community and not indulge their own consciousness to such a degree that they become very rarified, like Henry James.

We have seen this struggle played out in the previous novels by Sarah, Emma and Rosamund, and Clara too struggles to find community.

There is also the influence of Evelyn Waugh's novel, *Brideshead Revisited* (1945), in which the middle-class Charles Ryder becomes involved, via college friendship, with the aristocratic Marchmain family, and learns to appreciate 'the baroque'. In conversation, Drabble has agreed with my suggestion that Clara's recognition that eagles on furniture can be beautiful and not necessarily pretentious parallels Charles's growth in appreciation of aristocratic style. Drabble characters also have Joycean 'epiphanies', visionary moments of insight, brief and fitful, into the meaning of things. Clara learns, through the Denham family, to see.

But the Marchmain family in *Brideshead* is flawed, in that bullying masquerades as love, Lady Marchmain has been damaged by her husband's desertion, and so have the children, and so forth. The Denhams are also meant to be less glamorous in the eyes of the reader than they are in Clara's, but it is not easy for the reader to see quite why. The creativity of the parents has not descended to the children, but are the parents necessarily to blame for that? Margaret Drabble has said to me, 'those people are surely phoney, though, aren't they?' I must confess I find in the Denham family the same romantic charm as Clara does, and as I find in Drabble's own Hampstead milieu (which in its mirrors and general ambience is remarkably like the Denham house in Highgate as described; indeed, Drabble's own house has fortuitous romantic associations in that it backs on to Keats's house and is built at what was formerly the bottom of Keats's garden, presumably haunted, in those days, by nightingales). We do not see or hear much of Sebastian Denham, who is described as a poet, but we meet his wife Candida, unaffectedly 'posh' as Rosamund is posh, an attractive woman, a successful writer with grandchildren. That the children are not equally successful seems to be due to the fact that they have had 'uncritical affectionate encouragement', and their parents gave them arty names. But Clara

> . . . had never . . . seen or heard of such a mother, a mother capable of such pleasant, witty and overt concern, nor had she ever seen an image of fraternal love. She had read of it in the classics, as she had read of human sacrifices and necrophilia and incest, but she had not thought to see it with her own eyes.

For Clara, normal family affection is as remote and unknown as the darker activities of humankind (though where in 'the classics' do we find necrophilia?). Poor Clara has had neither affection nor encouragement, and falls in love (as does Charles Ryder in *Brideshead*), with a whole family, a common enough phenomenon in disaffected adolescents. Sebastian Flyte in *Brideshead* and Clelia in *Jerusalem* become quasi-siblings for the protagonists. Charles Ryder comes, like Clara, from a family which is cold and heartless, though Waugh was drawing on his own chilly father, and Drabble was drawing on her maternal grandmother. It would have been easy to let the girls, Clara and Clelia, meet at London University, but Clelia, despite being (we are told) brilliant and original, does not seem to have gone to college; she has wandered, with parental encouragement, round Europe, as has Clara. Clara's journeys are tragi-comic: a student of French and Spanish, she has had to 'fight' her mother for permission to travel. Both girls seem to have lost their virginities abroad,[5] and Clelia is involved (romantically? sexually? the point is unclear) with her married employer, whose wife has left him. Clelia's boss, Martin, has left her literally holding his baby, which she meekly takes in. Clelia, who has fulfilled the desire of her parents for her to be 'strange and wonderful', does not even have much of a job—her days are spent sitting at a desk in Martin's gallery, reading because of the paucity of visitors. The 'golden nest' does not propel the five Denham children out into the world: the eldest has married and gone dotty, the untalented Magnus has become a workaholic, Gabriel has married unsuccessfully, and Clelia and Amelia are still at home, though it is time Clelia left. But Drabble's unease with the family seems to have literary roots rather than conviction that there is something necessarily wrong with having wealthy, cultured and indulgent parents.

I first read the account of Clara's life with a shock of recognition: how did Drabble, the child of graduate parents, educated at boarding school, know my story, even to the Sunday School prizes in the attic, the coloured glass door panels, the dead father in insurance? We get little of Mrs. Maugham's conversation; our knowledge of her comes via one of Drabble's favourite techniques, retrospective narrative summary, which suggests that the experience of such mothering came to her at second-hand. The portrait is nevertheless cogent enough.

> [Mrs. Maugham] had been brought up as a chapel-goer, and two generations back her family had been staunch Wesleyans, but she herself . . . now considered all religious observation as ridiculous *frivolity* [italics added]. . . . the narrow fervours and disapprovals were there, but their objects had subtly altered over the years.

Susanna Wesley believed that to spare the rod was to spoil the child, that children should be constrained to 'cry softly' and that the prime object of upbringing was to 'break the child's will'. Fifty years ago, British mothers were warned severely by 'experts' of the dangers of 'spoiling', and many mothers, in those days, bent so far backwards as to be harsh.[6] Mrs. Maugham tells the story of the Christmas stocking filled with ashes, as a lesson. This story is probably a folk tale, but I too heard it in childhood: children had to be broken in to a harsh world, taught that those who expected nothing would not be disappointed. Mrs. Maugham tries to persuade her children that spending money is to be equated with 'vulgarity', and erects her own narrow prejudices into moral principles, with total lack of consistency or even rationale. She is a widespread British type: under-educated, soured by disappointment, self-righteous, censorious, seeking cheap moral superiority in a vain bid for status. May Maugham is the 'kind who turns down grammar school places' because uniforms have to be bought, and Drabble has to wrench the plot slightly to permit this anti-intellectual woman, who treats her daughter with 'venom' and 'malice', to let her go to Paris on a school trip at all. The problem is solved by allowing Mrs. Maugham a careless moment of acquiescence, followed by endless grumbles about expense. But she takes a characteristic revenge on her daughter, spoiling Clara's victory by making her wear a dowdy, if originally expensive, cast-off party dress. The anguish of being forced, at 16, to wear such a garment is unimaginable to those who have not lived through such experiences. At every stage, Mrs. Maugham has derided and undermined her clever daughter; instead of praising her budding good looks, she can only sneer, 'Handsome is as handsome does.'

Presumably Drabble believes that Clelia's mother is too indulgent and Clara's is not indulgent enough. Clara seems to have been an unwanted child: she was named Clara, then an unfashionable name, 'as a preconceived penance', though her 'only offences at that tender age were her existence and her sex'. She is christened out of 'a characteristic mixture of duty and *malice*' (italics added). Clara's childhood is wretched: she has 'affection in her and nowhere to spend it'. Even after getting to university, she dreads the vacations, and a return to the 'trembling, silent, frustrated anxiety . . . endured throughout her childhood'. She is haunted by 'guilt and hate and sorrow', fearing manic depression and schizophrenia. Her life is one of 'meanness and humiliations', and Clara's friends tell her she should 'clear out quick, be ruthless, cut all ties'. Clelia wisely refuses to give advice, except to suggest that Clara might do a postgraduate course in education, which will give her an extra year in London. Here the plot creaks slightly: Clara never seems to have any lectures to go to, let alone teaching practice; within the terms of the novel, she continues to lead the carefree life of an undergraduate. She has a 'director of studies', as though she were at Cambridge.

Critics are divided as to whether or not Clara is likeable. Drabble has expressed anxiety about Clara's future: 'She's going to turn into something fearsome, I think.'[7] Susanna Roxman has pursued the parallels between *Jerusalem the Golden* and Thackeray's *Vanity Fair*, first noted by Michael Ratcliffe and myself [Roxman, p. 25], and Lynn Veach Sadler has valuably traced references to Bunyan throughout

Drabble's work. I am indebted to Roxman for the suggestion that Clara's vision of her future at the end is an aspect of Vanity Fair: it glitters, but is not true gold.[8] Indeed, how can one see 'the glassy institutions' on the motorway where Clara envisages 'eating eggs and chips' with Gabriel in a kind of eternity other than a cheap and limited version of heaven? Nora Foster Stovel has traced, in *Margaret Drabble: Symbolic Moralist*, and in an important essay in *Margaret Drabble: Golden Realms* (ed. Schmidt), the continuity and coherence of Drabble's imagery of gold. Stovel writes:

> Most critics see only Clara's social success and fail to perceive her moral failure: even Virginia K. Beards, in her intelligent article, 'Margaret Drabble: Novels of a cautious feminist', *Critique*, 15, 1 (1973), p. 43, judges Clara successful in gaining 'deliverance from her humdrum provincial background'. The only critic to comprehend fully Clara's moral failure is Ellen Cronan Rose. . . .[9]

This is a valid, even important, point. However, while it may be a moral failure to dream of being rescued by a married lover instead of staying with a mother about to die of cancer, there are mitigating circumstances. Clara has been greeted not with warmth, or reconciliation: her mother speaks to her 'bitterly, sourly', 'fretfully', 'with all her ancient venom'. Clara knows that there is no hope of 'reconciliation, some gleams of sympathy or need'; she does not want her mother to show any 'chink' in her 'stony front'—she can only 'answer meanness with meanness'. The best Clara can do is to offer her mother a transfer to a private nursing home, but her mother lies defiantly that after three weeks' treatment she'll be 'fit to go home', though they both know she is dying. Clara is partially redeemed, after this appalling deathbed conversation in which the truth is not faced and familial affection is denied, by an epiphany: she hears two grey-haired women talking fondly about their grandchildren, and recognizes that, even in grim Northam, love and warmth are possibilities.

> And she felt once more charitably towards herself, that she had had no wish to hate; she had merely wanted to live.
> She visited her mother again in the evening. . . .

Here one feels Clara should be congratulated on her resilience and courage, rather than condemned for her failure. Her author has described Clara as 'her most unsympathetic heroine' and does 'not *like* her very much'; she is 'go-ahead, lively, a grabber'.[10]

As Joanne V. Creighton puts it, the reader is 'pushed into an uneasy mixture of sympathy for and condemnation of Clara's determination to escape'.[11] Critics are now agreed on the novel's moral complexity.

Although the Denham household has dying flowers, an empty hearth and pretentious artefacts in the garden, it is a 'golden nest', an alternative vision of childhood. Drabble has loaded the dice against the Denham family's quasi-incestuous intertwining. Annunciata has lost this warmth, but in one sense, dislocated as she now is, she is luckier than Clara, who never had it.

Margaret Drabble's view of Wordsworth's *Immortality Ode* is relevant:

> He does his best to close it on a note of optimism . . . but nevertheless what comes across most powerfully from the poem is a feeling of anguished regret for what is lost. . . . resolution . . . can never make up for what is gone, and he knows it.[12]

Over-civilized, over-protective though it is, the world of the Denhams has value; Clara sees that Candida's photograph album is a record of love, and even though Clara does not learn to love, she eventually recognizes, in her own city, love's possibility. The instinct that propels her towards an understanding of the love that has been denied her can only be healthy. Clara shows a possibility of moral development, even though it is not actualized within the novel.

Ellen Cronan Rose considers this to be Drabble's 'first wholly realized novel' in which she is 'completely in control of her material'. Rose's chapter on it and its relation to Arnold Bennett (discussed later by Drabble when she came to write his biography) is essential reading.[13]

NOTES

1. These echoes have been explored by Nora Foster Stovel, Lynn Veach Sadler, Susanna Roxman and Ellen Cronan Rose. Rose relates Ellen Moers's analysis of Christina Rossetti's poem, 'Goblin Market' in *Literary Women* (pp. 153–61), to Drabble's own references to the poem in Clara's consciousness. Rose finds a 'strong odour of perversion that clings to the Denhams'. Clara, in Rose's words, 'elects to join the family and share its life of incest' (Rose, p. 43, n. 6). It is worth noting, however, that both Emma Evans and Rosamund Stacey seem attracted to the idea of incest.

2. For authoritative discussion of these developments, see M. H. Abrams, *The Mirror and the Lamp* (Oxford: Oxford University Press, 1953), p. 159 ff.

3. Cooper-Clark interview, reprinted in Rose, *Critical Essays*, p. 25.

4. Ibid., p. 27.

5. Critics argue about whether or not Clara is a virgin when she first has relations with Gabriel on his office floor, but she has often thought of her mother previously, 'when drunk or naked', and she agrees with Clelia that British girls 'go abroad for their sentimental education'. These hints suggest she is not.

   When I set up Drabble studies at the Beijing Institute of International Relations in 1988, at the invitation of the Chinese government, my students were shocked at the sexual mores of Drabble's women. I was told that in China both parties are expected to be virgin at marriage and that illegitimacy is a rare disgrace; in China Rosamund would have had an abortion.

6. Before Benjamin Spock advocated more relaxed mothering, orthodox child-rearing favoured rigidity; Rosamund mentions Truby King, a New Zealand doctor who taught that babies must not be rewarded for crying by cuddles or rocking, but must be left alone, that feeds should be at four-hourly intervals, without so much as a minute's deviation, and that children's hands should be tied with splints at night to prevent masturbation. This advice was anxiously followed, in the interests of 'discipline', considered essential from birth.

   My late friend Professor A. M. Wilkinson did not wholly accept my account of life in the northern lower-middle class half a century ago; he said that he experienced no such 'mean parenting' as I write about. However, Drabble herself (Cooper-Clark interview, reprinted in *Critical Essays*, p. 22), says: '. . . it's much easier to be a good parent now than it used to be. In England, family life was frigid and rigid and difficult. Nowadays . . . it's much more flexible.' In the British Council interview tape she made with me, Drabble said that the book was about 'the particular kind of dour northern life that I was brought up on. . . . I still have this feeling that something in me was permanently squashed. . . .'

7. Interview with Nancy Hardin, *Contemporary Literature* 14 (1973), 273–95.
8. Nora Foster Stovel recognizes it as 'a tinsel fantasy' (*Margaret Drabble: Symbolic Moralist*, p. 90).
   Ellen Cronan Rose points out: 'Drabble uses light imagery to define Clara's aspirations and then undercuts them by associating with the dominant light imagery a verbal motif of coinage, which underscores Clara's ruthlessness in the pursuit of her golden dream' (*Margaret Drabble: Equivocal Figures*, p. 31).
9. Schmidt (ed.), p. 18, n. 18.
10. Interview with Iris Rozenswajg, *Women's Studies*, 6 (1979), 335–47.
11. Joanne V. Creighton, *Margaret Drabble*, p. 67.
12. Margaret Drabble, *Wordsworth*, Literature in Perspective (London: Evans Brothers, 1966), p. 123.
13. Ellen Cronan Rose, *Equivocal Figures: The Novels of Margaret Drabble* (London: Macmillan, 1980), pp. 28–48.

5

The Waterfall (1969)

Superficially, this fifth novel marks a return to Drabble woman (Oxford graduate, married, a young mother), struggling to find a new morality and sanctify adultery, with doubts, despairs, diffidences. Formally, it marks an advance, in that it is mildly experimental. Drabble has famously said she would rather be at the end of a dying tradition she admires than at the beginning of one she deplores.[1] To anticipate, Lore Dickstein, reviewing *The Realms of Gold* in the *New York Times*, 16 November 1975, p. 5, said 'her style is closer to George Eliot's than to Virginia Woolf's.' Near the time she wrote *The Waterfall*, Drabble came to read Virginia Woolf with new appreciation, having previously objected to Woolf as snobbish and precious. Virginia Woolf had declared war on Bennett, H. G. Wells and John Galsworthy, the Edwardian novelists, and in a famous passage in *The Common Reader* Woolf accused them of being

> . . . materialists . . . they are unconcerned not with the spirit but with the body. . . . they write of unimportant things. . . . they spend immense skill and immense industry making the trivial and the transitory appear the true and the enduring. . . . look within and life, it seems, is very far from being 'like this'. Examine for a moment an ordinary mind on an ordinary day. The mind receives a myriad of impressions—trivial, fantastic, evanescent, or engraved with the sharpness of steel. From all sides they come, an incessant shower of innumerable atoms; and as they fall, as they shape themselves into the life of Monday or Tuesday, the accent falls differently from of old. . . . Life is not a series of gig lamps symmetrically arranged; life is a luminous halo, a semi-transparent envelope surrounding us from the beginning of consciousness to the end.

This became an unofficial manifesto of what has been popularly called 'the stream of consciousness'. Experimental novelists, such as Woolf (1881–1941), James Joyce (1881–1941), and in our own day Thomas Pynchon (born 1937) are studied in universities, but have made little impact on the middlebrow reading public. My contention in my earlier book, *Margaret Drabble: Puritanism and Permissiveness*, was that Drabble is a highbrow writer with a shrewd commercial sense, an intellectual wolf in middlebrow sheep's clothing. Few Drabble scholars would now dispute this. My students in Beijing asked of every Western writer, 'Is he social realist or is he a stream of consciousness?' While these categories no longer seem adequate, Drabble's novels make modified use of the 'stream of consciousness', especially in the first-person narratives; but the fertilizing effect of reading Woolf freed Drabble, in *The Waterfall*, to reconcile the empiricist tradition of Bennett with the subjectivity, sensitivity and symbolism of Virginia Woolf. It is this decision that contributes to *The Waterfall*'s split narrative, alternating between first and third-person, its image of a split psyche, in which the mind and the flesh 'must meet or die', and its dominant image of that great wet cleft, Gordale Scar.

In 'Granite and Rainbow' (1929), Virginia Woolf wrote:

> . . . it is in poetry that women's fiction is still weakest. It will lead them to be less absorbed in facts and no longer content to record with astonishing acuteness the minute details which fall under their own observation. They will look beyond the personal and political relationships to the wider questions which the poet tries to solve—of our destiny and the meaning of life.

As I have argued in the earlier book, 'our destiny and the meaning of life' are Drabble's preoccupations from her earliest work, even when her narrators seemed to be 'absorbed in facts' (Emma Evans collects facts about the Angevin Empire, Rosamund Stacey collects facts about Elizabethan sonnet sequences, remaining 'wholly uncreative'; Clara Maugham too seeks and acquires information). Drabble has never neglected the 'personal and political relationships', but in *The Waterfall* she considers, within her narrative frame, the various meanings of 'romance' and 'romantic love'. *The*

Waterfall is on one level that common genre, the 'nervous breakdown novel', as is Woolf's *Mrs. Dalloway* (1925). In *Mrs. Dalloway* the main character, Clarissa, is a fashionable hostess, but the dark underside of the novel shows us her *alter ego*, Septimus Smith, shell-shocked and victim of the psychiatric profession, who eventually commits suicide (as did Virginia Woolf herself, in 1941). Different critics import their own preoccupations into their readings of Drabble: Ellen Cronan Rose finds widespread anorexia, I find a tension between agoraphobia and a longing for community, and also a preoccupation with madness and suicide. But when I suggested to Drabble that Jane in *The Waterfall* was suicidal, the author was sceptical, though she admits to having had Sylvia Plath and her recent suicide in mind. Drabble once met Sylvia Plath, but did not know her well.[2] *Mrs. Dalloway* is explicitly echoed, in that Jane, like Mrs. Dalloway, has a 'virginity preserved through childbirth'; both are compared to nuns. Virginia Woolf wrote in her workbook, 'Mrs. D. seeing the truth. SS seeing the insane truth.'

Jane's lover accuses her of being mad (though Drabble denies, in her interview with me, that any of her characters is clinically mad). But Jane the first-person narrator struggles with neurosis to create a picture which encompasses both a romantic fiction and truth to experience.

Michael Harper, in a suggestive essay on Drabble, writes:

> Unlike the Moderns . . . post-structuralists do not believe that language can be made isomorphic with a Reality which exists and is available independently, but maintain that our 'Reality' is constituted by language. . . . The enterprise associated principally with the name of Jacques Derrida thus claims not merely that language is always an interpretation of reality but that the reality to which language supposedly refers is itself an interpretation, a writing, rather than a 'given' present to our senses. . . .[3]

In 1969, these ideas, now commonplace, were beginning to be talked about in universities. It has become a critical cliché, now, to say that the subject of a particular fiction is not society or character, but the associated problems of *écriture*. Whether or not Drabble consciously apprehended these concepts in 1968–69, they inform *The Waterfall*. Jane

61

Gray, the protagonist, is said to be a poet, but we get no examples of her verse; she is struggling to convert the sometimes unsavoury facts of a quasi-incestuous love affair with her cousin's husband into a poetic novel, commenting on her own struggle, her own failures as a writer, to tell the truth. Drabble's prose has previously been crisp and analytical; here, she uses poetic symbol, sweeping poetic prose rhythms, with unprecedented richness. On her interview with me, Drabble said:

> I remember agonizing . . . a great deal: it's a sentence about Psyche and how she looked at Cupid. And she says: 'When she had returned the sleeping baby to [the] cradle she leant over him once more,' him the man James, 'touching his hair, his face, but he started to stir so she turned from him instantly, afraid to wake him: afraid that all his revealed beauty might vanish if he caught her surreptitious vigil or that he might be taken from her for her too great solicitude, as Cupid was from Psyche when she dropped on him the molten wax.' When I wrote that, I thought that's very poetic, and very true. . . . Then I thought that's a bit too poetic, so I switched the word order around and I put 'as Cupid was from Psyche' (that's poetic, it's inverted), 'when she dropped the molten wax on him', and I thought, that's better, that's more realistic. Then I typed that out, and then I looked at it again and I thought, no, I'm afraid this is an artificial sentence, it's a poetic sentence and it'll have to be 'dropped on him the molten wax'.[4]

This contradicts the often repeated statement that Drabble rarely revises. She added: 'I look back with the literary critical eye . . . that was so ferociously over-trained, and see what I did, but I couldn't actually plan how to do it beforehand.' She also said:

> I wouldn't like to be a poetic novelist in the sense that Virginia Woolf is. I admire Virginia Woolf enormously, but I would rather that there was a more real, normal level of experience, and level of prose going through the novel than Virginia Woolf ever provides one with, and so in a way, I think I'm flattered that people don't think the novels are poetic. . . . when you construct a plot, you are thinking, oh, Henry James did this, or Henry James did that, or Angus Wilson did this. . . . I do find, when I'm writing, I have to avoid reading certain people because they have such a powerful influence on me, because,

inevitably, one starts imitating them . . . sometimes one can do a conscious imitation, or a conscious parody, and hope that the discerning reader will pick it up and know what you're doing. But, if you don't want to do them, it's very difficult to find your own voice.

The Waterfall is partly about a novelist, brooding on Keats, Jane Austen and Charlotte Brontë, struggling to find her own voice. Around this time, Drabble had read Elizabeth Smart's novel, *By Grand Central Station I Sat Down and Wept*, which is a digested influence in *The Waterfall* in that it is narrated by a woman with a married lover, in a fractured non-sequential narrative which makes, ultimately, a kaleidoscopic pattern, without final resolution.

Lorna Irvine writes of Jane's

> . . . self-conscious discussion of the craft of writing. In the final section, this discussion focusses not only on possible endings for *The Waterfall* itself, but also on theoretical issues pertaining to the status of endings in general. . . . By contravening fiction's attachment to death, by denying the stringent calvinistic causal formula . . . [the novel] dramatises a philosophical rejection of predestination . . . pointed illustrations of her characters' freedom to make choices affirms the dignity of the human struggle.[5]

I would add that in asserting this freedom Drabble also rejects Woolf's psychology of perception, making the writer's mind not the recipient of impressions, but active in perception and the struggle to explore, in fiction, antinomial truths. The talcum powder in the whisky glass, alluding to the powder dissolved in wine from the legend of Tristan and Isolde, a story of doomed love, flippantly subverts the conventions of romantic love, while affirming their subjective validity.

As Nora Foster Stovel puts it:

> *The Waterfall* is the most intensely subjective and symbolic of Drabble's sixties novels, because she uses symbolism as a psychological tool for probing the psyche's individual vision and for tracing its development, as the self is delivered from the artistic womb of the imagination into the real world of reason.[6]

Stovel adds that water is used as the central symbol of love because it nourishes humanity as water refreshes vegetation, and can be frozen or melted.

The images are of blood, milk and water, semen, the female secretions, the liquids inside 'our stiff bodies'. *The Waterfall* is romantic in the sense that, as in the work of the romantic poet Percy Bysshe Shelley (1792–1822), the poet-heroine-narrator is a divided self, seeking reintegration. The split narration, which Drabble says occurred as a result of technical problems, but which turns out expressive, is, of course, not Drabble's invention: it goes at least as far back as Charles Dickens's novel, *Bleak House* (1853). Yet the two narratives are here put to original use, discriminated: the third-person narration flows smoothly, conventionally; the first person narration is a partial commentary on it, with disrupted, hesitant, interrogations, representing the inner mental turmoil behind the narrative facade. Jane writes:

> He redeemed me by knowing me, he corrupted me by sharing my knowledge. The names of the qualities are interchangeable: vice, virtue; redemption, corruption; courage, weakness; and hence the confusion of abstraction, the proliferation of aphorism and paradox.

The novel's key concept is a favourite paradox of medieval philosophy, the organic link between 'generation' and 'corruption'. Sir Thomas Browne writes of 'that axiom in philosophy that the generation of one thing is the corruption of another'.[7]

Rosamund, in *The Millstone*, persuades herself she holds 'an Aristotelian, not a Platonic, view of fiction'. Aristotle and Plato were Ancient Greek philosophers, who continue influential after two and a half millennia. Plato condemned fictions as untrue and likely to set bad examples; Aristotle replied that 'poetry is more philosophical than history', because poetry (that is, literature), deals with universals, whereas history deals with particulars. Historically, Aristotle's has generally been the more popular view, but Plato's other legacy, immensely seductive to artists, is his belief that the phenomenal world is only a reflection of a transcendent reality. This Platonic strain is discernible in the poet William Blake (1757–1827), when he wrote in his notebook:

This world of Imagination is the world of Eternity; it is the divine bosom into which we shall all go after the death of the Vegetated body. This World of Imagination is Infinite & Eternal, whereas the world of Generation, or Vegetation, is Finite and Temporal. There Exist in that Eternal World the Permanent Realities of Every Thing that we see reflected in this Vegetable Glass of Nature.[8]

Drabble characters frequently catch sight of reflections in or through glass: Jane Gray, trapped in a moment of waiting for her lover, watches the 'soulless fishes' swimming in their glass prison and thinks of eternity, saints and visionaries. *The Waterfall* is permeated with rot, mould, decay, cockroaches, dust, sin and death. Jane's house is collapsing, the body imaged as prison of the soul. She has struggled to describe '. . . the pure flower of love itself, blossoming out of God knows what rottenness, out of decay, from dead men's lives, growing out of my dead belly like a tulip'. (This recalls Swift's 'such gaudy tulips grow from dung'; Drabble's work is honeycombed with such covert literary references. The reader is expected to recognize the image of the albatross from Coleridge's poem 'The Ancient Mariner', and to recognize a brief allusion to Alfred Lord Tennyson's poem, 'Mariana', to supply the information that Mariana waited for her lover at a moated grange in Shakespeare's play, *Measure for Measure*, to spot that 'cold pastoral' comes from Keats's poem, 'Ode on a Grecian Urn'.) Bunyanesque word-play is made with the words 'generation' and 'corruption' in multiple senses: 'They were of my generation, like me they were corrupt' (the narrator is thinking of original sin, of human nature, the irredeemable 'savagery' of which she 'fears'). 'All of her was for healing. . . . Ah, never, damaged from birth, beyond repair, damaged before birth, an inheritance of afflictions.' On the literal level, Jane has just given birth to a new 'generation', and childbirth is followed by new sexual love (reversing the normal order). Her sexual salvation 'merely stressed for me the dreadful, sickening savagery of human nature'. Jane's 'deliverance' is ambiguous and multiple in its resonances. She is delivered of her child, delivered from her sexual frigidity and into divine grace through this sinful, corrupt and fleshly love which yet redeems her, as love must, in 'that strange sobbing cry of rebirth'. This release into love, out of painful agoraphobic isolation, is Jane's 'ghostly resurrection'.

Her salvation is real, yet her lover, James, has more than a whiff of the demonic. He is her temptation. He appears to her 'lovely, like a flower, like an angel', seems to display 'angel-like simplicity', yet he 'always told elegant lies', like the devil, who is the father of lies. Jane, like Eve, is tempted, but her fall brings 'knowledge' and makes redemption possible. Yet the fall brought 'death into the world and all our woe' in John Milton's great religious poem, *Paradise Lost* (1667), an important influence on later literature. James is mentioned as in bed, a small boy, with a 'wicked' mother. Is it too far-fetched to think of him as death, son of Satan and his daughter Sin? Drabble has said herself in conversation, 'the end of romantic love is death', and James comes from Norway. In medieval tradition, the north is where the fallen angels come from (possibly because of Isaiah, 14:12, 13). James is associated not with the organic, which in Drabble's work represents 'great creating nature', but with motor racing, with the mechanical. James 'seemed to carry with him the yellow sulphureous clouds of some threatening imminent disaster', he is 'an appallingly dangerous driver, religiously consistently dangerous, passionately bad'. The racetrack has a 'curious *sulphureous* [italics added] burning smell', which for Jane is 'the smell of sex and death'. Jane thinks James has taken her there 'to frighten her, to torment her, to make her suffer for him'. The racing cars in James's garage are 'a menace of death', and he drives her down Death Hill. James says, 'I like it hot' and 'I like it here because it's so hot.' He smokes a whole packet of cigarettes in one evening, making the room 'dense with smoke'. We are reminded of the demonic Alec D'Urberville in Hardy's novel, *Tess of the D'Urbervilles* (1891), imaged by a glowing cigar. Hardy's novels *Tess* and *Jude the Obscure* (1895) are, like *The Waterfall*, about the conflict between flesh and spirit, played out in triangular sexual relationships. Jane, ironing, burns a hole in her son's shirt, when James returns; James's 'skin burned her'; she writes of the 'burning smooth flesh of his shoulder'. He is 'a dangerous man', with 'pale fanatic eyes'.

She becomes 'addicted' to the sight of him. He neglects his family, never does any real work, and after the accident there is a smell of pitch, which, according to the Bible, 'defiles'. Tackled about his idleness, he replies, delightfully: 'I'm what's called a sleeping partner.' He tells Jane he spends time with her because of 'boredom . . . Because really, I've got nothing else to do.' Even his skill with card-tricks is a 'sinister dexterity'.

Yet the mews where James works is

> . . . full of budding foliage; there were plants in window boxes, and creeper climbed past the double doors, putting out their small new leaves. They decorated the mechanical paradise, they made it live and grow.

Vegetation, the natural world, are contrasted with the icy wastes of Jane's loveless life, abandoned by her husband, before James becomes her lover. Jane's fall is, like Adam's, fortunate, a *felix culpa*, and the symbol of grace and redemption is Gordale Scar (mis-spelled by Drabble and commentators as 'Goredale', just as the poet Campion is mis-spelt 'Campian') where

> . . . the water leaps down through the side of the cleft pouring itself noisily downwards across brown rocks that are twisted and worn like wood, like the roots of the trees.

Overflowing water is the traditional symbol of the blood of Christ shed for us, pouring from the wound in his riven side: 'Rock of Ages cleft for me', as the hymn by the Rev. A. W. Toplady has it. Blood and water are multi-faceted symbols in this novel. Gordale Scar is a split rock, and in traditional symbolism 'dual rocks are a celestial doorway giving access to another realm.'[9] Gordale Scar is truly the 'waterfall' of the title, evidence that grace is real.

Gordale Scar is in Drabble's native Yorkshire, and a famous beauty spot. Any regular visitor to London's Tate Gallery is familiar with the magnificent painting by James Ward, an example of the eighteenth-century sublime, a real 'romantic chasm' to quote Samuel Taylor Coleridge's poem, 'Kubla Khan' (1816). There is also the famous description (1770) by the poet Thomas Gray (1716–71), author of the famous 'Elegy in a Country Churchyard':

> . . . a stream that at a height of about fifty feet gushes from a
> hole in the rock, and spreading in large sheets over its black
> front dashes from steep to steep, and then rattles away in a
> torrent down the valley. . . . one black and solid mass . . .
> overshadows half the area below with its dreadful canopy. . . .
> I stayed there (not without shuddering) a full quarter of an
> hour. . . .

Wordsworth wrote one of his less successful sonnets on it.
Drabble writes, in *A Writer's Britain*,

> . . . any post-Freudian would of necessity see this landscape
> in terms of sexual imagery—the hollow cavern, the gushing
> water, the secrecy of the approach, the tufted trees—and
> would remark how notably this vocabulary is missing from
> Gray and Gilpin, though it is present enough in John Milton,
> whose references to the womb of waters, to genial moisture, to
> heaving mountains, laps and entrails and bosoms, to shaggy
> hills and bushes with frizzled hair and hills with 'hairie sides',
> make the creation of the world sound a thoroughly sexual pro-
> cess: he sees the world as a living being, conceived, gestated,
> born, passing through unadorned childhood to the springing
> tender grass of puberty. This organic vision was lost for a
> century and a half after Milton: it was deeply inaccessible to
> Gray and his contemporaries. (p. 129)

Milton's poem 'Lycidas', about drowning and water, themes
integral to *The Waterfall*, is alluded to in passing: 'Comes the
blind Fury, while I am in anguish, deciding whether to peel
or scrape the potatoes. . . .' And Jane's ink, pouring on to the
sheets like blood, her 'sublime blood', recalls Milton's dictum
that 'A good book is the precious lifeblood of a master spirit'
(*Areopagitica*, 1644).

The overt allusion in *The Waterfall* is to George Eliot's *The
Mill on the Floss* (1860), another novel about symbolic water.
Jane, like Maggie Tulliver, pinches her cousin Lucy's man,
but whereas Maggie's adventure results in renunciation,
followed by death, Jane clings on to James, who has survived
his car accident. The tormenting of the small boy whose
father is a Labour candidate by Jane's father, headmaster at a
prep school, parallels the teasing of Maggie Tulliver's brother
Tom by the Reverend Mr. Stelling (Bk. 2, Ch. 1). ('Maggie' is
Drabble's own nickname, incidentally.) In *The Waterfall* Lucy

is a sort of twin, the same age as Jane, and although Jane has a
real sister, Catherine, we hear little about her, and Lucy fulfils
the rôle of sister-rival-*alter ego*, though in this case it is not
certain which sister wins dominance. Jane wonders whether
or not she wants James 'because he was hers, because I
wanted to be her'. Lucy and Jane, like sisters, share a bed in
a hotel while James is in hospital.

There are other, fainter, literary echoes. In Charlotte Brontë's
last novel, *Villette*, the heroine narrator, Lucy Snowe, wins her
man, Paul Emanuel, from the jealous clutches of his cousin,
Madame Beck. The religious phrase 'living water' is used by
Lucy Snowe to describe Paul's letters, and by Jane Gray to
describe the reviving effect on her of James's lovemaking. And
The Waterfall owes much to Virginia Woolf's *To the Lighthouse*
(1927), which is about an artist's vocation, and in which the
sea is a dominant symbol, in particular of femininity and
creativity.

Despite Jane Gray's existential agonies and her rejection
of Jane Austen's morality, the Jane Austenish laughter is still
there: Jane's and Lucy's mothers complain of the selfishness
of char-women who refuse to work on Christmas Day, and
reminisce, resentfully,

> . . . about past betrayals, about char-women falling sick on the
> eve of dinner parties, about butchers neglecting to deliver vital
> joints of meat, about gardeners deserting for more lucrative
> pastures and more tasteless rockeries.

Jane has married Malcolm 'to deny' her own 'Jane Austen
distinctions of refinement and vulgarity. . .'. But this attempt
at reaction does not succeed; her depressing parents-in-law
do not represent 'the cosiness and warmth of working-class
life. . . . Their style was arid and unlovely in the extreme.'
The brief sketch of Jane's interaction with her in-laws is
brilliantly comic, though neither narrator seems conscious
of this aspect. Jane considers her own feelings to be 'fascist
sentiments, fascist evasions'. Feeling this way is evidence of
Jane's leanings towards egalitarianism; 'Why should I have
suffered so from the terrible knowledge of inequality?' She is
politically confused, rejecting her parents' conservatism, yet
unable to embrace socialism. Yet her language betrays her as

one of nature's capitalists: it is loaded with the imagery of banking, credit, profit, loss, gambling, losing, winning.

The picture of Jane's loveless marriage, in which sex seems to be painful, is so appalling, it wounds the reader. The act of marrying is compared to laying one's head on the block, like Jane Gray's near-namesake, Lady Jane Grey, or jumping from a high window: 'a commonplace sacrifice'.

Jane finds love outside her marriage. Drabble, interviewed by Olga Kenyon, said of women's writing: 'Women have not thrown away the notion of the romantic novelist, romance, the dark stranger, love.'[10] Out of traditional, even corny, materials, she weaves a richly symbolic narrative. On one level, Jane's is a commonplace story of adultery. On another, it ponders creativity, femaleness, fertility, the nature of love, God, the uses of literature. It enacts the struggle to make art out of experience, drawing on ancient mythologies, medieval legend, Shakespeare, Woolf and Plath, a tapestry of fable addressing artistic, existential, theological and metaphysical questions in prose which shows a new depth and suggestiveness of texture.

In it, too, we find imagery which is to recur in later novels: isolation is imaged by dryness, craters, rocks, hilltops; life is imaged by greenery and the eternal rebirth of springtime; community and fulfilment are represented by immersion in the river of life, swimming with the current.

NOTES

1. Bernard Bergonzi, *The Situation of the Novel* (London: Macmillan, 1970), p. 65.
2. Sylvia Plath, American poet and novelist, committed suicide in London. Plath's biographer, Anne Stevenson, writes of Plath's 'perennial myth of rebirth', her despair, her preoccupation with her own gift, her images of blood and corpses. Plath's husband, like Jane's, left her with two small children. Plath had also resolved to be 'stronger' than Virginia Woolf, to live not 'for life itself: but for the words that stay the flux' (Anne Stevenson, *Bitter Fame: A Life of Sylvia Plath* (Houghton Mifflin, 1989: Penguin, 1990), p. 113).

Sylvia Plath, poet (1933–63) uses the image of Lazarus, who was raised, according to the Christian New Testament, by Jesus Christ from the dead. This image is also used by Jane Gray and the English woman poet, Elizabeth Barrett Browning (1806–61), in her semi-autobiographical novel in verse, *Aurora Leigh* (1857).

3. Michael F. Harper, 'Margaret Drabble and the Resurrection of the English novel', reprinted in Ellen Cronan Rose (ed.), *Critical Essays*, p. 57.

4. Roberta Rubenstein explores the mythical antecedents in her essay, '*The Waterfall*: The Myth of Psyche, Romantic Tradition, and the Female Quest', in Dorey Schmidt (ed.), *Margaret Drabble: Golden Realms*, p. 139–57.

5. Lorna Irvine, 'No sense of an ending: Margaret Drabble's continuous fiction', specially comissioned by Ellen Cronan Rose (ed.), *Critical Essays* (p. 77). This essay, deservedly celebrated, is a convincing answer to those like Donald Davie, who in his review of *The Ice Age* in the *New York Review of Books*, 10 November 1977, criticized Drabble for writing 'a book that one has to call a novel, though it is written as if [Henry] James had never written his agonized disquisitions about, and experiments in, composition and the narrator's point of view'. Joanne V. Creighton takes a similar view to Davie's, preferring the earlier novels as more tightly constructed. But as Drabble told me in interview, it is her ambition to write what James condemned as 'loose, baggy monsters', because they are more true to life, and she prioritizes life over art.

6. Nora Foster Stovel, *Margaret Drabble: Symbolic Moralist*, p. 96.

7. Sir Thomas Browne, *The Vulgar Errors*, III, ix. Sir Thomas (1605–82) was a Norwich physician. *The Vulgar Errors* (1646), according to the *Oxford Companion to English Literature*, ed. Margaret Drabble, is 'his most learned and ambitious work'.

8. William Blake, *A Vision of the Last Judgement*, from the notebook, pp. 69–70.

9. J. C. Cooper, *An illustrated Encyclopaedia of Traditional Symbols* (London: Thames & Hudson, entry under 'Rock'). The entry under 'Water' fills three columns, but includes: 'All waters are symbolic of the Great Mother and associated with birth, the feminine principle, the universal womb, the prima materia, the waters of fertility and refreshment and the fountain of life'—all meanings present in the novel.

10. Interview with Olga Kenyon, in *Women Writers Talk* (Oxford: Lennard Publishing, 1989), p. 29.

6

The Needle's Eye (1972)

The Needle's Eye seems a traditional novel, in theme, structure and ethical position. Of all Drabble's books it is the one which those admirers of hers who would like to find a place for her work within radical feminist politics have the most difficulty in coming to terms with. Most critics conclude that it is a work of 'conservative feminism'. Yet I side with the minority who consider it to mark a radical disjunction from her previous work and to be radical, too, in its sexual politics, though not in an obviously recognizable way. *The Needle's Eye* reverts to the omniscient narrator, yet despite what looks like familiar material (unhappy woman, mother of three, neurotic withdrawal), *The Needle's Eye* is a daring statement of radical feminism in the theological sense.

It is the least autobiographical: the heroine, Rose, who inherits and gives away a fortune, bears a striking resemblance to Margaret Drabble's friend and fellow-writer, Nell Dunn, who did just that; and when Rose's divorced husband, Christopher Vassiliou, snatches the children and threatens to leave the country, Rose is afraid he will behave like Mr. Calvacoressi, who had snatched a child and taken it to Italy. Mr. Calvacoressi is based on a Monsieur René Desmaraults, a French father who kidnapped his daughter Caroline from his former wife, who eventually regained custody of the child through the courts. The name Calvacoressi comes from one of Arnold Bennett's friends.

Marion Vlastos Libby has called *The Needle's Eye* a 'truly great contemporary novel, perhaps on a par with the best of Doris Lessing'.[1] The comparison with Doris Lessing is suggestive, for this is an attempt to tackle wider themes than hitherto. Doris Lessing is no stylist, and in this novel gone are the epigrammatic, polished, balanced sentences of the earlier works: now the sentences are long and rambling, often with commas where the reader might expect full stops. The repeated use of the northern inversion, with subject pronoun followed by verb, which is followed by a noun subject (e.g., 'he might as well lose his eyes, man') occurs in the speech of all characters, not only those from the north, but also in that of southerners, in whom such idiom would be folksy affectation, and is used by the omniscient narrator. The effect is one of (deliberate?) clumsiness (compounded by copy-editors who failed to correct mis-spellings such as 'payed' and 'prophecying'). The old Evangelical-Methodist concept of a 'serious person' is solemnly invoked. Lynn Veach Sadler considers this to be Drabble's 'first greatly serious novel'.[2]

However, it upset Drabble's admirers. As Sadler neatly puts it:

> The women's liberation movement has embraced her and rebuked her. . . . Drabble has travelled a long way from being embraced as the champion of motherhood and nappies—though her children were always facts to be dealt with, never characters as such.[3]

In the novel, Rose is a battered wife, having suffered bruises, split lips and other injuries at the hands of her enraged husband. At the end of the novel, she takes him back, denying her own spiritual development, for the sake of the children, to whom he has never offered violence; it is his love and concern for them that determines Rose's decision. Feminist critics found Rose's capitulation shocking. Husbands, in the Drabble canon, resort to violence: David Evans in *The Garrick Year* and Malcolm Gray in *The Waterfall* smash things, bash their wives' heads against walls and floors. The return of Christopher is not a hopeful prospect for Rose, as Drabble holds a Freudian, deterministic view of character: she has repeatedly said that people cannot change, or 'not very much'.[4] The relationship between Drabble and her feminist readers has never been comfortable: Ellen Cronan Rose demanded 'a feminist blueprint',[5] and rejected Drabble's 'conservative message' of 'self-denial, renunciation, an equation of womanhood with gritting one's teeth and bearing it'. Drabble, interviewed by Olga Kenyon, supplies a partial answer:

> I was interested, talking to students in Hamburg, that the word feminist has a much more hostile connotation . . . it means you are an active campaigner. . . . If one doesn't know the reverberation of a word in another country one can't know what one is implying when saying, as I usually do, 'Yes I'm a feminist but.'[6]

The word feminist, like the word 'puritan', has subtly different connotations in Britain from those obtaining in America. It is no coincidence that two articles have rubricated her feminism as 'cautious': Diana Cooper Clark's interview is titled, 'Margaret Drabble: Cautious Feminist' and Virginia Beards's essay is called 'Margaret Drabble: Novels of a Cautious Feminist'.[7]

In manner, the novel reverts to the nineteenth century, recalling Dickens's *Dombey and Son* (1847), *Bleak House* (1852–53) and *Hard Times* (1854), and Mrs. Gaskell's *North and South* (1855). In *The Needle's Eye*, the story-line is reversed: unlike Gaskell's Margaret Hale, a southerner who learns to understand the life of the north, Simon Camish, a northerner like Drabble herself, becomes reconciled to life in Hampstead. Both *North and South* and Mrs. Gaskell's earlier *Mary Barton* (1848) deal with Trade Unions. Simon is a member of a Fabian socialist firm of barristers, and he specializes in union law. And Simon's visit to 'Violet Bank', a dismal industrial area, and his conversation with the old woman about the ruined countryside recall the reminiscences of old Alice, the herbalist, in *Mary Barton* (Chapter 4). Drabble's old lady has no such traditional skills, only memories of a better day.

The Needle's Eye is schematic, full of parallels and antitheses. Interviewed by Diana Cooper-Clark, Drabble mentioned Wordsworth's 'spots of time in one's life when one is in touch with something slightly beyond the immediate . . . the transfiguration of the everyday'.[8] *The Needle's Eye* is full of these: Simon's visions in the garden, which veer dangerously near cliché; Rose's walk in London after the rain. Lynn Veach Sadler remains unimpressed:

Perhaps Drabble chooses to see all and tell all in her novels and yet tell nothing because, for all of her contemporaneity, she floats atop old themes in old ways (e.g., symbol, epiphany, emblem, microsmic, macrocosmic, analogy, Freudianism).[9]

Sadler brilliantly analyses the Bunyanesque allusions, yet her opinion is surprising: earlier, she has written, 'One of the beauties of *The Needle's Eye* is that, so much in the mode of Bunyan's allegories, it is yet so unallegorical. . .'.[10]

Nora Foster Stovel recognizes that the custody suit is merely the 'surface conflict'[11] of the novel. She observes that 'Simon's mother and Rose's nurse are both cut from the same Calvinist cloth as Clara's mother.'[12] Stovel recognizes that 'The key to Drabble's moral meaning is not so much in the surface vehicle of the action as in the underlying symbolism . . . in her most allegorical novel yet.'[13]

Drabble herself has said, 'I think the idea that you are here to enjoy yourself is very wrong. You're here in order to do the right thing and to seek the depths in yourself. . . .'[14] *The Needle's Eye* is nothing less than an exploration of what it means to be good. Christopher is redeemed by his care for his children and by his economic activity: serving Mammon, he serves God by love of children, a dubious equation. Politically, the book is uncommitted, like the Victorian 'condition-of-England' novels it recapitulates; like Mrs. Gaskell, Drabble suggests that society's ills can be put right not by laws and trade unions, but by redeeming love. Rose, challenged by her father, denies involvement with the Communist party. Unlike Simon, she is not a declared socialist; the roots of her behaviour are religious, not political. She hopes to 'do good' by giving away her money, by seeking out the dispossessed and living in a squalid working-class district. Yet although she minds Eileen Sharkey's illegitimate baby occasionally, she never identifies with the uneducated poor she lives among; at the end, she confesses to herself that her gesture in refusing to live among her own social equals in Hampstead had 'lacked community'. Rose never does a proper job, although she potters for a while in the launderette. As a speaker she is ineffectual, and she never becomes actively involved in neighbourhood welfare. She is concerned, instead, with her own soul, and it is not clear whether we are to admire her or condemn her for this. The climactic moral paradox, by which she sacrifices her peace to live with a wife-beater, does violence to our own moral sense. The question as to whether Christopher's divorce has cured his bad habits remains unaddressed. Rose goes downhill after the reconciliation. Drabble's novels are full of unresolved ambiguities; she loves irony and paradox, resists closure.

Simon's own socialism is not carried over from his profession to his personal life; all he feels, apart from a vague intuition that it is wrong for people staying in expensive hotels to condemn men in overalls for wanting higher wages, is a hope that the tree will be shaken so the superflux goes to them. Quotations from Shakespeare's *King Lear* are recurrent in Drabble's work. He feels guilt as a 'masquerader' because he was not born in the professional classes. Despite Drabble's own professed socialism, the book's tenor is conservative, taking the line that not of this world is the Kingdom. Christopher attacks Rose for her mad, 'wicked' idea of trying to be good; he does good without meaning to, according to the parable of the talents (Matthew's Gospel in the Christian New Testament, 18: 24). In Matthew, 7: 1 we find 'Judge not that ye be not judged.' (The parable of the sower, Matthew, 13, was invoked in *Jerusalem the Golden*.) From Matthew, 19: 24 comes the novel's thematic key: 'It is easier for a camel to go through the eye of a needle, than for a rich man to enter the kingdom of God.' Rose's son, Konstantin, accuses her of being a 'whited sepulchre', a phrase from Jesus's attack on the Pharisees (Matthew, 23: 27). The novel is full of references to houses built on sand (see Matthew, 7: 25, 27). Simon, Rose, Emily and their children go for a walk in London after rain. They see a hen and chickens on a bombsite. Lynn Veach Sadler relates this passage to *The Pilgrim's Progress*, Part II (1648), in which Christiana and her friend Mercy, travelling to the Celestial City, are shown by the Interpreter a hen and chicks as an emblem of God's love. This association comes from Matthew, 5: 37:

> O Jerusalem, Jerusalem, thou that killest the prophets and stonest them which are sent unto thee, how often would I have gathered thy children together, even as a hen gathereth her chickens under her wings, and ye would not!

Simon feels a 'great and innocent peace', 'like the rainbow after the flood' (see Genesis, 9: 13). Bunyan and the Bible are the structural principles of *The Needle's Eye*: 'Let your light so shine before men that they may see your good works. . .' (Matthew, 5: 16). Rose subscribes to an ancient orthodoxy, a modern heresy: she believes in faith, as well as in works. Christopher is justified by works. Rose tries not to lay up treasures on earth (Matthew, 6: 19, 20). John 3: 8 is quoted: 'The spirit bloweth where it listeth.' Rose's epiphany about 'the harsh clanging of her own voice, the sounding of righteous brass and the clanging of the symbols of her upright faith-demented ideologies' is a punning reference to the words of St. Paul, 1 Corinthians, 13: 1: 'Though I speak with the tongues of men and of angels, and have not charity, I am become as sounding brass, or a tinkling cymbal.' Directly quoted we have St. Paul, 2 Corinthians, 3: 5, 'The letter killeth, but the spirit giveth life'—a proposition Simon, to whom the law is livelihood, disagrees with. The point of the novel is that while both are needed, neither is adequate by itself, and they can be mutually incompatible.

The Needle's Eye is clearly more than a story about a marriage. Drabble herself has compared *The Needle's Eye* with other novels about rich young women and the use of wealth, such as Henry James's *The Portrait of a Lady* (1881), *The Wings of the Dove* (1902) and *The Golden Bowl* (1904). Nora Foster Stovel notes echoes of James's *Washington Square* (1881) and *The Princess Casamassima* (1886). (It may be coincidence that Rose's two instalments of 'thirty thousand pounds' repeat the inheritance Elizabeth Barrett Browning's heroine, Aurora Leigh, repudiates when she refuses, initially, to marry her cousin, Romney Leigh.[15]) Stovel quotes Drabble's reply to Joan Mannheimer: 'One of the themes I was trying to explore was the possibility of living, today, without faith, a religious life.'[16] In the same article, Drabble asserts that the novel's logic demands that Rose remarry Christopher. (And in Henry James's *The Portrait of a Lady*, Isobel goes back to her wicked husband.)   Susanna Roxman relates Rose's morality to Immanuel Kant's 'deontological ethics', citing H. J. Paton's *The Moral Law: Kant's Groundwork of the Metaphysic of Morals* (1948):

. . . the moral worth of an action does not depend on the result expected from it, and so too does not depend on any principle of action that needs to borrow its motive from this expected result.[17]

In other words, Rose takes Christopher back because Christopher has a moral right to his children. It is her duty. Roxman chooses to interpret 'faith' as deontological ethics and 'works' as utilitarianism. Roxman denies that Rose is 'religious':

. . . she is not sure whether God exists or not; except for moments of crisis, she does not appear to think about God at all, and never goes to church or chapel.[18]

Roxman writes:

Carol Seiler-Franklin asserts that Rose 'Willingly . . . gives up her own happiness hoping thus to ensure other people's.' . . . such considerations are not relevant to Rose's moral outlook.[19]

Rose's 'religion' would seem to be more complicated than Roxman acknowledges; Rose's anxieties are due to Noreen, her hellfire-breathing nurse. Roxman does not consider whether such anxieties are soundly based, a question posed by the novel. Sidestepping the issue, Roxman distinguishes between religion and ethics. This makes partial sense, yet Rose's concern with grace can hardly be described as other than 'religious'. Throwing off Noreen's life-denying brand of religion, Rose decides 'to hell with Bunyan' and settles for a 'heroic neurotic nonchalance'. Yet her final resolution to 'leap off the ladder even blindfold into eternity, sink or swim, come heaven come hell', is an echo of Bunyan's *Grace Abounding*. Roxman argues that Simon is certainly not a religious person. His emphasis on 'purposes, not results . . . might be called deontological'.[20] Roxman points out that Christopher's ethics are more 'utilitarian', but that neither Rose's nor Christopher's ethics are ultimately wholly rejected by the end of the novel.[21] The recognition of unresolved ambiguity is well taken. Roxman quotes a letter from Drabble, dated 14 June 1978, which endorses Roxman's reading.[22]

Arnold E. Davidson recognizes that Drabble is 'deliberately equivocal about the import of the religious themes so regularly sounded'.[23] Rose and the other characters are 'pilgrims without progress', but 'pilgrims still. And therein lies their hope for the future.'[24] He relates the novel to Trollope in its plotting and to George Eliot in its concern with 'noble spiritual promptings and the necessarily imperfect reality of partly achieved vision. . . . *The Needle's Eye* can be seen as both an advance and a retreat from the prevailing mode of modern British religious fiction.'[25]

Drabble told an interviewer: 'What I wanted to do was have the reader see what each felt about the other and where they had got each other wrong, which I admire tremendously in other people's books.'[26] She told another interviewer: 'I don't know what my images mean, but I know they mean something fairly involved to me and I use them because I don't know what I mean in words.'[27] Drabble's material here and in earlier works is the permanent spiritual plight of mankind. In *The Needle's Eye* she ponders the paradoxes of Christian theology, familiar in bygone ages, now esoteric, to illumine that plight. Her continuing preoccupation with the tension between flesh and spirit, sin and grace, between the phenomenal world and the transcendental, here produces a novel so heavily allegorical that the social world seems meagrely realized within it. Matthew's Gospel underpins the whole, for both texts are a series of parables, dealing in puzzling ways with the paradoxes of material and spiritual wealth and the Kingdom of God. 'Whoever will lose his life for my sake shall find it. For what has a man profited, if he shall gain the whole world and lose his own soul?' (Matthew, 16: 25, 26). Rose arguably reverses this concept: she sacrifices her soul to gain the human world, to live 'in dispute and squalor for the sake of charity and of love'. As Arnold E. Davidson comments:

> The rationale rings false . . . Rose and Christopher are, at the end, essentially the same characters that they previously were and are as unhappy in their reestablished marriage as they were in the original one.[28]

This form of self-sacrifice, not the rejection of her children or the giving of money to Africa, is the heroic gesture demanded of Rose.

As a child she had imagined herself to be a reincarnation of Jesus Christ. We are invited to see Rose as at least in part a Christ-figure: like Christ, she sacrifices herself for her children, for humanity. But in becoming more human, Rose loses her vision of the Celestial City. The reference is to Bunyan's *The Pilgrim's Progress*; the novel quotes directly, as we have seen, from his *Grace Abounding*. Rose's heavenly city looks back to St. Augustine's City of God, the heavenly city of Revelation in the Bible, and Plato's archetype in *The Republic*, Book IX:

> *Glaucon*: The city we have been describing has its being only in words, there is no spot on earth where it exists.
> *Socrates*: No, but it is laid up in heaven as a pattern for him who wills to see, and seeing to found the city for himself. Whether it exists anywhere, or ever will exist, is no matter.

This passage, says F. M. Cornford, inspired both Stoics and Christians with the idea of a City of God. Rose as a child has a school friend Joyce (is there an allusion to James Joyce, the celebrator of Dante and the mystic Rose, the epiphany?) The two children have a favourite word, 'Yonder'. Only the learned reader is likely to be aware that 'Yonder' was an important concept for the mystical Neoplatonists of the early Christian era.

Barbara Dixson, who identifies twenty-six explicit Bible references,[29] points out that Rose's name is symbolic, going back to the Biblical Song of Solomon and reaching a medieval peak in the vision of the mystic rose at the end of Dante's *Divina Commedia*, where it 'embraces Mary, Paradise, grace and Divine Love, and at the same time reconciles these spiritual concepts with the hitherto opposing concept of terrestrial courtly love.'[30] (The unconsummated love between Simon and Rose is a modern version of courtly love.) The meanings of the rose are almost inexhaustible; according to J. C. Cooper's *An Illustrated Encyclopaedia of Traditional Symbols*, the rose is

> . . . a highly complex symbol . . . ambivalent as both heavenly perfection and earthly passion, . . . time and eternity, life and death, fertility and virginity . . . perfection . . . completion; the mystery of life; the heart-centre of life . . . beauty, grace; happiness, but also voluptuousness . . . wine, sensuality and seduction.
> In the symbolism of the heart the rose occupies the central point of the cross, the point of unity. As the flower of the

feminine deities it is love, life, creation, fertility, beauty . . .
death, mortality and sorrow; its thorns signify pain, blood and
martyrdom . . . it portrays eternal life, eternal spring, resurrection . . . it is the flower of Venus and the blood of . . . Christ
. . . the Rose Garden is a paradise symbol . . . Alchemic: the
rose is wisdom . . . the rebirth of the spiritual after the death
of the temporal . . . the flower of paradise . . . from the drops
of Christ's blood on Calvary . . . the centre of the rose is the
sun and the petals the infinite, but harmonious, diversities
of Nature. The Rose emanates from the tree of Life, which
implies regeneration and resurrection.[31]

All these meanings are applicable to the figure of Rose within
the novel. Her first appearance associates her with ancient
religious verities:

> She looked, because of age and softness, authentic, as ancient
> frescoes look in churches, frescoes which in their very dimness
> offer a promise of truth that a more brilliant (however beauti-
> ful) restoration denies.

Rose brings healing to Simon—'It was nothing less than a
rebirth in his nature'—and the white rose in his winter garden
becomes a mystic symbol for him, during the progression
from winter to spring, symbolic of spiritual renewal. Simon
is even granted a vision of Rose, haloed in glory:

> . . . the bright air, and her hair itself, falling on to the
> points of her fur collar, fell into a thousand bright individual
> fiery sparks, the hair and the fur meeting, radiant, luminous,
> catching whatever fell from the sun upon them, stirring like
> living threads in the sea into a phosphorescent life, turning
> and lifting . . . a million lives from the dead beasts, a million
> from her living head, haloed there, a million shining in a
> bright and dazzling outline, a million in one. She walked
> ahead, encircled by brightness.

Clearly here Rose is a saint or divinity, possibly even *Rosa
Mundi, Stella Maris,* the Queen of Heaven ruling the stars.
Compare Matthew, 15: 13–15: 'Ye are the light of the world. . . .
Let your light so shine before men that they may see your good
works, and glorify your father which is in heaven.'

When Rose, as implied narrator, commits profanity, there
is usually a concealed, orthodox religious undertone: 'Christopher, Christ, she had to admit that Christopher would have

got life from a stone'; '. . . in ten years one could look back and say, Christ, how could I have done that?' She is pondering mistakes believed to be at the time 'acts of truth and faith and righteousness'. Consider, also, '. . . French schoolboys who burned themselves to death as a protest against what's going on in Biafra, as a protest, for Christ's sake, as a sacrifice to the French oil wells'. Rose tries to be one of 'the poor in spirit' (Matthew, 5: 3). She agrees that 'Strait is the gate and narrow is the way' (Matthew, 7: 14). Attention is drawn to Rose's middle name, 'Vertue'. Her married name is also important: 'Vassiliou' means 'son of Basil'; Basil, in Greek, means King or Lord.[32] Rose, her husband Christopher, bearer of the Christ-child on his shoulders, and their children are all children of the Lord, God in man and man in God. Rose, like Christ, represents both humankind and the godhead within the human breast (cf. Luke, 17: 21, 'The kingdom of God is within you'). Simon, Rose's disciple, sees her as 'the human, the lovely, the stuff of life itself'. She carries within her, too, something of the holy. Rose, like Christ in Matthew's Gospel, undergoes a temptation in the wilderness: she thinks of renouncing her children. Like a sacrificial victim, she constantly bleeds; she feels her brain is 'wet with blood . . . I bleed, I bleed, I bleed. Let them not tell me we are material beings, it is in the spirit that we know pain. . . .' She treads on a broken ketchup bottle and cuts her foot; she cuts her thumb with a razor, drawing blood; she slashes her wrist, releasing 'huge red wet drops the size of pennies'. This passage recalls Dame Julian of Norwich and her vision of Christ crowned with thorns: 'great drops of blood rolled down from the garland like beads. . . '.[33] Julian's writings emphasize the motherhood of Christ: 'I saw that there were these three attributes: fatherhood, motherhood and lordship—all in one God.'[34] Christ, for Dame Julian, is 'our mother also in mercy, since he has taken our sensual nature upon himself . . . in our Mother, Christ, we grow and develop.'[35]

The association of Rose, motherhood and the Incarnation is supported by the image of Simon's own sacrificing 'pelican-like' mother who had 'fed him with her own blood'. The pelican, tearing its breast to nourish its young, is a familiar image for Christ. On the literal level, every mother nourishes her embryo with her blood. Motherhood (especially in Drabble's work) is a form of redeeming love, a sacrifice of blood and suffering: every mother, in her divine power of bringing forth new life, has something in her of the Creator, re-enacts the Incarnation, love made flesh. Drabble's position would seem to be the neo-Gnostic one as defined by Sir Norman Anderson: the Incarnation is 'interpreted as a process ever-lastingly being accomplished within the souls of all men and women'.[36] Anderson adds that women, as mothers, are especially privileged. One might add that, conversely, every birth may be seen as a new Incarnation, every family a holy one. Rose is divine by virtue of her motherhood; her intuition that she is 'Christ reincarnated' is not mistaken.

Drabble is writing in a mode older than that of secular humanism, older than that of modern scientific empiricism. In her novels, these modern world-views are criticized. Simon is a 'devoted empiricist', 'an unbeliever', yet his outlook is modified by his association with Rose. In her family rose-garden he sees

> The lake of disaffection, the spring of hope, the alleys of reunion. Once in Oxford, on a summer night, he had looked out of his bedroom window across the college gardens, awakened by a dry thunderstorm, and there lay the garden, formal, beautifully maintained, lit by ray after ray of a pale, amazing watery green, each leaf picked out, each flower blanched with immortality, everlasting flowers, and through the garden wandered, lit also by these fabulous shafts of light, the oldest fellow in the college . . . gathered up together in some . . . delusive allegory of the soul.

For Simon the unbeliever, such allegory is necessarily 'delusive', yet we are to understand that his vision is limited to the here and now. Drabble is using the medieval mode of religious allegory in which symbols do not have a one-to-one correspondence, but, as we have seen in the example of Rose Vertue Vassiliou herself, interpenetrate and reflect one upon the other for spiritual teaching.

Rose's daughter is called Maria; Rose represents 'love, life, creation, fertility', the mother of mothers-to-be, the mother even of the mother of God (one thinks of Milton's 'fairest of her daughters, Eve' in *Paradise Lost*). She is related to the pre-Christian era and the female chthonic deities, true earth mother, child of Nature and of the Lord, partaking of the human and the divine. Far from showing that Drabble has 'regressed'[37] in this novel, as Ellen Cronan Rose believes, *The Needle's Eye* is a daring statement of radical feminist theology. Rose's motherhood is to be read as creativity, sacrifice, identification with the numinous and with nature; without knowing it, she reconciles flesh and spirit, though this knowledge is concealed from her. Her identification with Jesus Christ is no childish fancy, for in Christ's humanity every human being may find a reflection, and as Dame Julian puts it, Christ is our Mother.

NOTES

1. Marion Vlastos Libby, 'Fate and Feminism in the Novels of Margaret Drabble', *Contemporary Literature*, 16, No. 2 (1975), 176.
2. Lynn Veach Sadler, *Margaret Drabble*, p. 62.
3. Sadler, p. 131.
4. E.g., Creighton interview, published in Dorey Schmidt (ed.), *Margaret Drabble: Golden Realms*, p. 22.
5. Ellen Cronan Rose, *Equivocal Figures: The Novels of Margaret Drabble*, pp. 128–29.
6. Kenyon, p. 31.
7. Virginia Beards, 'Margaret Drabble: Novels of a Cautious Feminist', *Critique*, 15 (1973), 35–47.
8. Interview with Diana Cooper-Clark, reprinted in Ellen Cronan Rose (ed.), *Critical Essays*, p. 25.
9. Sadler, p. 120.
10. Sadler, p. 62.
11. Nora Foster Stovel, *Margaret Drabble: Symbolic Moralist*, p. 120. In 'Margaret Drabble's Golden Vision' (in Dorey Schmidt (ed.), *Margaret Drabble: Golden Realms*, p. 3), Stovel writes: 'Enthusiasm over the high recognition level of Drabble's social realism, however, has blinded most critics to the poetic imagination beneath the surface verisimilitude. . . . Her use of symbolism is the key to the other side of her genius, the poet beneath the realist, and raises her fiction above the level of mere social realism to the realms of poetry.'
12. Stovel, p. 116.
13. Stovel, p. 110.
14. Cooper-Clark interview, reprinted in *Critical Essays*, p. 20.
15. Elizabeth Barrett Browning, *Aurora Leigh*, a novel in verse (1857).

16. Margaret Drabble, 'The Author Comments', *Dutch Quarterly Review of Anglo-American Letters*, 5 (1975), 37.
17. Susanna Roxman, *Guilt and Glory*, p. 128.
18. Roxman, p. 133.
19. The reference is to Carol Seiler-Franklin, *Boulder-Pushers: Women in the Fiction of Margaret Drabble, Doris Lessing and Iris Murdoch*, European University Studies, Series XIV, Anglo-Saxon Language and Literature (Berne and Las Vegas: Peter Lang, 1979).
20. Roxman, p. 135.
21. Roxman, p. 143.
22. Roxman, p. 128.
23. Arnold E. Davidson, 'Parables of Grace in Drabble's *The Needle's Eye*', in Dorey Schmidt (ed.), *Margaret Drabble: Golden Realms*, p. 73.
24. Ibid.
25. Schmidt (ed.), p. 67.
26. Interview with John Clare, 'Margaret Drabble's Everyday Hell', *The Times*, 27 March 1972, p. 6.
27. Interview with Nancy Hardin, in *Contemporary Literature*, Vol. 14, No. 3 (Summer 1973), 273–95.
28. Arnold E. Davidson, in Dorey Schmidt (ed.), *Margaret Drabble: Golden Realms*, p. 71.
29. Barbara Dixson, 'Patterned Figurative Language in *The Needle's Eye*', in Dorey Schmidt (ed.), *Margaret Drabble: Golden Realms*, p. 133.
30. Dixson is quoting Barbara Sweard, *The Symbolic Rose* (New York: Columbia University Press, 1960), p. 3.
31. J. C. Cooper, *An Illustrated Encyclopaedia of Traditional Symbols* (London: Thames & Hudson, 1978).
32. I am grateful to Alison McRobb, of Cambridge, for this information.
33. Dame Julian of Norwich, *Revelations of Divine Love*, trans. Clifton Wolters (Harmondsworth: Penguin, 1966), p. 72. Dame Julian (1342– c. 1416) was a religious hermit, who wrote about her visions. Her current fame derives from T. S. Eliot's poem, *Little Gidding*, which quotes her: 'Sin is behovely; but all shall be well and all shall be well and all manner of thing shall be well.'
34. Dame Julian, p. 165.
35. Dame Julian, p. 166.
36. Sir Norman Anderson, *Christianity and World Religions: The Challenge of Pluralism* (Leicester: Intervarsity Press, 1984), p. 21.
37. Ellen Cronan Rose, *Equivocal Figures*, p. 91.

7

The Realms of Gold (1975)

The Needle's Eye can now clearly be seen as a watershed in Drabble's development. As I have argued in my previous book, the continuing preoccupation of the first six novels is eschatological, despite surface social realism. Jane Gray in *The Waterfall* is an unbeliever, yet she is obsessed with fate and necessity, and her vocabulary is of 'grace and miracles', despite her expressed dislike of such concepts. Grace comes to Jane through human contact after nun-like withdrawal. Drabble says she did not read Virginia Woolf until 1969. However, Jane's preservation of essential virginity, through marriage, through childbirth, is a direct echo of Woolf's *Mrs. Dalloway*, although *The Waterfall* appeared in that year. It seems likely that Drabble had already skimmed Woolf earlier, but only read her with appreciation and mature understanding at a later date. The question as to whether Rose finds grace or loses it is left open; but the Calvinist terrors of damnation suffered, in different ways, by Jane and Rose, and which were part of Drabble's own early adolescent experience, seem to have been laid to rest, and replaced by a 'heroic neurotic nonchalance'.

In our British Council interview, I said I found it disturbing that the most perceptive heroines, Jane and Rose, were driven nearly mad, and accused of being so by their menfolk. Yet they saw farther into existence than the positivists, rationalists and empiricists like Simon Camish and Rosamund Stacey.

Drabble replied:

> I think they do see further into existence but, on the other hand, I would like to point out that they do stay alive on

the last page, and none of them are clinically mad. . . . Rose does get near madness, but at the same time she never stops making cups of tea and making the beds: she copes, she's someone who will always go on coping. She may have terrible crises of depression and despair and spiritual anguish, but she will always remember that the children have to be got up and the socks have to be washed.

Olga Kenyon asked what led Drabble to start writing; Drabble said:

The startled astonishment that it was difficult to be free and a mother. My first three novels were written during my three pregnancies. . . . There were undercurrents of rage, though they are veiled compared to later writing. . . . This was the first time women novelists dealt frankly with subjects not considered 'polite', such as breastfeeding, hysterectomy, wanting too much. . . .[1] I was not conscious of myself as a woman writer. Then I realised there were parallels with Victorian novelists: I was bored, lonely, needed money. I had no sense of conscious feminism. I began modestly with no encouragement, or discouragement, from anybody. In a tradition which includes Jane Austen and George Eliot there is no need to feel apologetic . . . a conventional university education gave me confidence in my opinions. I had been taught to think for myself, not parrot others, both at school and at university. . . . I thought I had a whole new world that other people hadn't written much about. . . . Also . . . I was a sort of prisoner. As the children grew older, I saw one could write a different sort of novel, do research, travel. I'm deeply ashamed that I could not travel while writing on Arnold Bennett. But the restraint is connected with the great joy of bringing them up.[2]

She adds that for *The Needle's Eye* she did research, attending law courts and meeting other people to get information.

Diana Cooper-Clark asked her, 'Various critics have perceived a formidable range of "isms" in your work—Calvinism, existentialism, empiricism, determinism, and nihilism. How useful do you find these terms in response to your work?'

Drabble replied:

. . . I try not to think about them. . . . I never sit down and think, 'Well, now I'll write about Calvinism or now I'll write about empiricism.' It's perfectly valid to spot bits of Calvinism in my work. But we could spot bits of Calvinism in almost anybody who'd ever read the mainstream books in English literature. I find the existentialist writers very arid. I'm quite interested in the people who write to me about freewill and determinism. But then, I'm not the first person who found that interesting; it's just an interesting question. I suppose on that level my novels are serious and that I do try and tackle some fairly serious subjects because I think about them a lot. But, to me, a book should be entertaining.[3]

Drabble is philosophically literate; the English literature course at Cambridge University examines knowledge of 'English literature, life and thought': awareness of the background in history and ideas is as important as knowledge of the texts. And Drabble elected to do a course in the philosophers, titled 'The English moralists', something of a misnomer, as the reading list includes Plato. She told Joanne Creighton: 'When I was at university, I was very interested in metaphysics and philosophy and now I've lost nearly all my interest in it.' Drabble added:

> I don't know if there is a final truth in Freudianism or in religion or in Marxism or in any of these interpretations or creeds. I don't know if any of them are a final truth. It's much easier to interpret the world if you believe in one of them and one only, but . . . I dabble in all of them and believe in little bits of all of them . . . they do cancel one another out, they don't add up. . . . I don't find myself able to commit myself to a line of interpretation that excludes the others.[4]

I would add that this is a very British stance, the product of centuries of Protestant eclecticism, in Drabble's case mediated through Nonconformity and its traditions of scrupulous examination of every tenet, as well as its preoccupation with searching the conscience. At the end of *The Needle's Eye*, despite Rose's painful capitulation to Christopher, we feel a sense of relief: Rose, returning to her origins, has had a partial revelation; the burden of religious anguish has dropped away, as Christian's burden drops away from him after his meeting with the Evangelist in *The Pilgrim's Progress*. The price Rose pays is the fading of her vision. The rise in the district of property values, the economic rebirth of the African country she gave the money to, reflect Carlyle's cyclic vision of history (Thomas Carlyle (1795–1881), the Scottish philosopher and commentator on the Industrial Revolution, was required reading at Newnham). This hopeful view of renewal after destruction and 'negation' was absorbed by Charles Dickens, whose work pervades Drabble's, though she denies being a Dickensian novelist. She told Olga Kenyon:

> I don't think I really am a Dickensian writer. The label got stuck because I'm interested in sociology and so was Dickens; and my novels are getting longer. I'm expected to do a Dickensian survey of London life. If only I could live up to it, I'd be happy.[5]

In *The Realms of Gold*, a title taken from the poem, 'On First Looking into Chapman's Homer', by John Keats (1795–1821), Frances Wingate is a free, successful woman, a distinguished archaeologist, her children off her hands, divorced, a traveller in the course of her absorbing work. If Frances has fears about predestination or hellfire, we never hear about them. But her very name gives us a clue to her anxieties: Francis Wingate was one of Bunyan's judges. And the novel opens with Frances in the grip of an attack of depression, or hysteria—whatever we call it, she endures the symptoms of nervous breakdown, which as we shall see runs like a virulent strain through her whole family network. Frances, like Clara Maugham in *Jerusalem the Golden* and Rose Vertue Vassiliou in *The Needle's Eye*, has to return to her origins to discover who she is and find a way forward. This is an irony, as Frances's profession is digging into the residues of other people and reconstructing their history from the evidence: bones, teeth, artefacts.

Frances works to ward off misery, which as she says leads her relatives to 'Suicide, drugs, drink, the madhouse'. In pain with a broken tooth, she thinks of 'the insufferable tooth decay of the ancient world'. Her head feels 'like a skull'. She thinks of herself as 'in the middle of nowhere, high up, a solitary lunatic, in her dry crater'. Her cure for pain is to repeat to herself poems by Milton and Wordsworth, which she has used to help her 'comply with her husband's desire for sexual intercourse' and which she had shouted aloud in childbirth. It is clear that her pain is not merely physical, but existential.

Her depression this time seems to be triggered by a memory of an octopus in a perspex box. Frances is aware that female octopods die after giving birth: she has given birth four times, and now wonders what else she is for. Taught to look on her miseries as cyclic, Frances, like Jane, expects revelation. Tranquillizers have had no effect. This is because she is not good at following instructions on bottles, or waiting for cumulative effects. The city she is in is deliberately vague: it might be Naples, it might be Marseilles. Frances, on a lecture-tour, has chosen to be solitary in her hotel room, because the city is where she finally parted from her lover, Karel. Karel is both weakling and saint, who gives his time and attention selflessly to others. Like Jane and Rose, Frances blames her 'wicked nature'.

> . . . something of a salvationist, he had wished to save her, with evangelical passion and she was afraid of disappointing him. . . . So she had told him firmly that she was mad and beyond redemption. . . .
> While not quite able to accept the theory of penis envy, she was more and more convinced that what every woman wanted was a man, and that what every man wanted was a woman, or that if they didn't want that they ought to, and that the only possibility of happiness and harmlessness on earth were to be found where Freud would have us find them.

The real problem is that Karel is married. Frances's own marriage has been grim and violent; it has hardened her, as isolation hardened Rose. Frances finds hope in 'the variety of earth's creation'. We have one of Drabble's memorable scenes: Frances recalls making love with Karel in a muddy field full of croaking frogs, a primaeval scene. Famously, she keeps Karel's discarded false teeth in her bra: 'One night at a party she caught a man . . . staring down her cleavage, and meeting, entranced and horrified, the sight of Karel's glaring teeth, the guardians of her virtue.' She cherishes 'teeth and bones' because Karel is Jewish and the only member of his family to survive the Nazis (we recall the grim heaps of relics).

The archaeological learning in the novel is impressive. Frances, like Schliemann who found Troy, has found, in 1968, a dead city in the Sahara called Tizouk. The knowledge of its whereabouts has come to her, after fitting together scraps of evidence, by intuition. Excavation leaves her anxious that she has pillaged the dead. Recalling Rosamund and Jane, 'She had been arid as a rock, but she had learned to flow.' Like Jane, Frances feels herself to be 'unnaturally powerful'. Reading Virginia Woolf's *The Years*, Frances remembers that the 'writer died young by her own hand'. *The Realms of Gold* is a sustained meditation on time, civilization and death. Virginia Woolf, in *Mrs. Dalloway*, writes of

> curious antiquaries, sifting the ruins of time, when London is a grass-grown path and all those hurrying along the pavement this Wednesday morning are but bones with a few wedding rings mixed up in their dust and the gold stoppings of innumerable decayed teeth. . . . (p. 19, Penguin edition).

On page 90, Woolf invokes the past:

> . . . when the pavement was grass, when it was swamp, through the age of tusk and mammoth, through the age of silent sunrise . . . the battered woman . . . stood singing of love. . . . As the ancient song bubbled up opposite Regent's Park Tube Station, still the earth seemed green and flowery: still, though it issued from so rude a mouth, a mere hole in the earth, muddy too, matted with root fibres and tangled grasses, still the old bubbling burbling song, soaked through the knotted roots of infinite ages, and skeletons and treasure, streamed away in rivulets over the pavement and all along the Marylebone Road, and down towards Euston, fertilising, leaving a damp stain.

Tree-roots appear regularly in Drabble's fiction and her prose rhythms in this novel are haunted by Woolf's. Frances wonders '. . . how had the first sowers ever learnt to trust the wheat to survive the winter? On such acts of faith has human life been built.' She thinks of the old Sahara: '. . . fertile, grass-covered and in places the hippopotamus had wallowed where there is no water for hundreds of miles.'

Her cousin, David Ollerenshaw, is a geologist. He is 'no conservationist: his aim was . . . the exploitation and not the preservation of the world's resources . . . man was merely another agent of change, like wind, or water, or earthquakes.' He regards alternative views as 'ridiculous'. Frances observes that the tribe of desert well-diggers are now employed in the oil industry. Working on the African continent, she identifies herself with Cleopatra. Shakespeare's play, *Antony and Cleopatra,* is mentioned in connection with messengers (a recurrent motif through this novel about trade routes, civilization and communication), and there is a submerged reference to Cleopatra's lament for Antony: 'His delights/ Were dolphin-like. They showed his back above/ The element they lived in' (Act V, sc. ii). David Ollerenshaw, on a Hebridean island, sees from a hilltop

> a sea full of small islands . . . raising their backs like dolphins from the water, heaving and burgeoning. . . . The landscape seemed alive, as though seething in the act of its own creation, for round every island the waves broke white and fell and glittered, in a perpetual swell and heave. The Isles of the Blest, he said to himself . . . and now they were going to dig it all up. . . . If the company sent him off to the Hebrides, should he on the grounds of conscience refuse?

David has a moment of revelation on the top of a volcano. David's idea of heaven would be to

> watch mountains heave and fold, seas shrink, rivers wear down their valleys, continents drift and collide, forests dry into deserts and deserts burgeon into forests. . . . Man's life span was too short to be interesting . . . in many ways, David was a typical post-Darwinian scientist, who had adapted himself without effort to the faith of scientific determinism: he saw order in the universe . . . what he knew of man did not justify his taking of any very dignified part in the scale of creation.

But he worries about irreversible change, wrought by nuclear physics. Perhaps there are other worlds, he thinks.

> David Ollerenshaw threw his cigarette end into the crater. The volcano received it, spewing gently from its blackened lungs, like a tired old prophet. It would not overwhelm him with its wrath.

The language is richly suggestive.

Unlike the Greek philosopher Empedocles (c. 490–430 B.C.), David does not throw himself into the volcano. Empedocles is the subject of a painting by Salvator Rosa (1615–73) and a poem by Matthew Arnold (1822–88). Discussion about him occupies three pages in Part III, among Frances's cultivated relatives. Although nobody in the novel knows what Empedocles's philosophy amounted to, it is relevant; according to the *Encyclopaedia Britannica*, he believed it was the philosopher's job to display the identity between what seem unconnected aspects of the universe. He attempted to explain the separation of elements by strife, the formation of the world. Originally animals had double sex, but were eventually reduced to two sexes and the world was replenished by organic life. 'This theory seems a crude anticipation of the modern "survival of the fittest" theory.'

Frances's parents come from the same stable as Rosamund's: chilly and academic. Her mother is a shrill proponent of birth-control and thus, we gather, anti-life. She comes from a family which collects Nobel prizes, while Frances's father is a scholarship boy, son of a small market-gardener. Sir Frank Ollerenshaw, professor of zoology, first developed his interest in science by studying newts. Drabble writes:

> Frances liked the newts best. They were elusive and therefore something of a sign of favour. One day she . . . had found several of the small ancient special creatures, floating on the surface, their little arms outstretched, taking the sun. Breathless, quiet, she sat there and watched them. They were surely a sign to her, a blessing. They floated there, green grey, pink bellied, frill backed, survivors from a world of pre-history, born before the Romans arrived, before the bits of bronze-age pot sank in the swamp, remembering in their tiny bones the great bones of the stenosaurus, a symbol of God's undying contract with the earth.

In her interview with me, Drabble said:

> . . . somebody, an American critic, wrote a very long analysis of *The Realms of Gold*, about how it was all about Darwin, and prefaced this analysis with a wonderful quotation from Darwin about the tangled bank. . . . And she said, 'It's unfortunate that Margaret Drabble made so many references to this passage from Darwin, because they stick out of the book'. But I'd never read the Darwin passage in my life . . . I have read some Freud, but these influences are so profound

that they obtrude if you happen to have read the source yourself. Whereas, if you haven't read the source, you don't see
it. I don't think that a reader who hadn't read Darwin would
notice that the tangled bank and the ditch was anything to do
with Darwin. . . . I originally intended this book to be . . . three
sections . . . equally long . . . to show three areas of British
life. . . . I did an O level correspondence course in geology . . .
and I wrote about thirty thousand words about my geologist.
And then . . . I realized . . . he was a convincing geologist,
but he didn't actually fit . . . so I cut him out, and then . . .
allowed a little . . . to creep in, because there were some bits
I couldn't bear to lose . . . my American publisher . . . wrote
back and said, 'What is this geologist doing in this book at
all?' . . . but I was determined to leave him in. So I then put
in a bit of authorial comment: I said, 'I had intended . . . to
make this character do X, Y and Z, but unfortunately I didn't
manage it. But there he is, and that's the answer to why he's
there: he just is there, because I put him there.'

I said:

> Yes, but . . . he works within the novel as well, because
> he represents the striving, the self-disciplined effort which,
> as you say in other books, is costly. But it's a very impor-
> tant part of civilisation and of evolutionary struggle up out
> of the mud, so your instinct to keep him in, I think, is
> justified.

Drabble said:

> There's a character in *The Needle's Eye* who is . . . in because I
> hated her, and I just put her down in a moment of fury. . . .
> I could justify David, the geologist, thematically: I could
> point out bits of imagery, I could point out things about
> the organic,[6] which is Frances's pursuit, and the inorganic
> which is David's pursuit. Well, that all works very nicely on a
> poetic, symbolic level. I'd also thought of integrating the plot
> by making him marry Janet Bird.

Janet Bird, née Ollerenshaw, another cousin on Frances's
father's side, lives a life truly awful, yet commonplace, on
a housing estate with a mean and arrogant husband. Janet
wants to stick a knife into him, for taking her from her 'safe
solitude'. Her only consolation is her baby, and like Jane Gray
she indulges in rituals of abnegation.

Drabble continued:

> They were also going to have had an affair in the past,
> and that would have integrated the structure: the plot would
> have stuck together if I'd made that happen. . . . A friend of
> mine . . . a novelist, read this book, and she said, 'I can see
> the point at which you thought, let's make Janet and David
> get married. And I can see the point at which you rejected
> it'. . . . She said, 'You wanted to give poor Janet, the
> downtrodden housewife, a little reward, didn't you?' . . .
> Really, what I'm saying is that no book is . . . anything
> like what you intended it to be, and when you're justifying,
> you're justifying after the event. While you're writing, you
> don't really know what you're doing, you're trying and
> attempting and constructing, and going down one path and
> going on another path. . . . *The Millstone*'s a very tidy book
> . . . there's something about *The Millstone* that I now find
> repellent, and it is precisely its coherence and tidiness. . . .
> It's the only one that isn't open-ended and it's the only one
> that hasn't got a lot of extra mess in it, and that is what I
> don't like in books. . . . [I like] the mud: the moving into
> the mud of existence. . . . Somebody recently described *The
> Realms of Gold* as an optimistic novel written by a confirmed
> pessimist. I think I'm pessimistic about human nature and
> human endeavour, and I think I'm pessimistic about the fact
> that we live in a world in which I wish God existed, and I'm
> afraid that God does not exist. . . . I, like Hardy, hope that
> God might be there, but I'm not at all sure that he is. Which
> is one of the reasons why I admire Hardy so much, because
> he expresses this feeling of despair, but hope, so wonderfully
> . . . in all my novels there's this gesture towards faith and
> towards belief in God, because I hope that God is there . . .
> the character who commits suicide, Stephen, cares so much
> for his baby that he kills his baby through too great a love,
> not through neglect or hatred, but because he loves the baby
> too much.

She added:

> . . . symbolism is not something that you . . . put in later,
> or dream up, or construct in your head. . . . Symbolism is
> something that comes so deeply out of you. . . . There's
> something in me that does think that if you go on hoping,
> and go on trying, and go on watering the spirit and feeding
> the spirit, then there must be some answer. We can't be

pessimistic, we can't despair. We can't reduce ourselves to silence and despair, because otherwise why would we have this profound need to nurture and keep ourselves alive?

The novel foregrounds Frances, rich and famous, while Janet Bird, miserable trapped housewife, is relegated to the sidelines. Arguably they reflect Drabble's later and earlier selves. At the end of the novel, Janet is 'biding her time' until something good happens for her, but given her circumstances it is hard to believe anything will happen for Janet until it is too late. We, too, would like to give poor Janet a little reward, but Janet's only hope is divorce and independence. Meanwhile, she has a young son. Her action in marrying is considered, by the omniscient narrator speaking through Janet's consciousness, in anthropological terms:

> What a crazy binge of objects a wedding produces. Insane. Tea sets, coffee sets, pyrex dishes with different designs, fish knives, ironing boards, toasters, electric kettles, what kind of refrigerator, what colour bedroom curtains. . . . There is some tribal insanity that comes over women, as they approach marriage: society offers pyrex dishes and silver tea spoons as bribes, as bargains, as anaesthesia against self-sacrifice. Stuck about with silver forks and new carving knives, as in a form of acupuncture, the woman lays herself upon the altar, upon the couch, half-numb. Even sensible women, like Frances Wingate. . . .

Such things became 'useless indestructible relics' (implicitly to be found by future archaeologists). Janet's mother wonders, 'Why didn't one drag one's daughters back from the altar, instead of pushing them up the aisle?'

The parable of the talents, of stony ground and the Biblical tag, 'To them that hath shall be given' (Matthew, 25: 29), are invoked in relation to lucky Frances and unlucky Janet. Janet entertains her husband's friends to dinner: they are 'in a conservationist phase' and think it smart to do without a car, so their friends have to drive them around. This observation possibly modifies our attitude to David Ollerenshaw, searching for oil. There is satire here: Janet has been brought up to think 'nice people voted Conservative', and cannot think what her husband and her guests, lecturers and managers, are playing at. They were all ambitious, they all had mortgages, they all complained about income tax, they all made jokes about working-class ignorance, so what were they doing voting Labour? . . . they were all delighted when the Tory council invited them to functions.

Dinner parties, communal meals, are, of course, symbolic rituals: 'What a funny business it was, dressing up in one's best clothes to go out to one another's houses to stare at one another's husbands.' The lights go out, reminding us how precarious is civilization. The talk turns to Iceni villages and the miracle of the first iron to be made, success invoked from deities rather than science. Eventually, 'The time had come to go home, to confront one's own ghost privately, one's own skeleton.'

Janet delays going to bed; she is satirical about the bright optimism of sex manuals, when all she can do is 'grit one's teeth and bear it'.

Even poor Janet has an epiphany:

> . . . she caught sight of the huge sky, which was an amazing colour, dark blue, with a foreground of dark pink and purple clouds, light but regular clouds, a whole heaven of them, spread like flowing hair or weed over the growing darkness. . . . The two colours were charged and heavy, and against them stood the black boughs of the tree at the end of the small garden, where black leaves, left desolate, struggled to fall in their death throes. The day before she had watched from the bedroom window a single leaf on that tree, twisting and turning and tugging on its stalk, in a frenzy of death, rattling dry with death, pulling for its final release. So must the soul leave the body, when its time comes. The amazing splendour of the shapes and colours held her there, the teapot in her hand. I will lift up mine eyes, she thought to herself. I should lift them up more often.

Janet finds beauty in nature and finds it consoling. Drabble said to Olga Kenyon:

> Wordsworth . . . means several things to me. . . . To this day I find him moving on the dignity of rather dull work, the dignity of motherhood. Also he writes about the natural world in such a way that one feels one can be restored for one's failure in human relationships. If I'm feeling really

depressed I go for a walk alone in the country, my heart lifts
up and I feel restored, a better person; it's a simple revelation,
but Wordsworth seems to be the first to have had it. How did
they manage so long without it?[7]

Frances in the book says the Romantics 'understood the
effects of landscape on the soul . . . frost at midnight,
and moon shone sweetly, and the formative influences of
a Lake District? Hartley, and all that?' She is alluding to
Wordsworth, to Coleridge and his poem, 'Frost at Midnight',
in which the poet apostrophizes his infant son, Hartley:

> . . . I was reared
> In the great city, pent mid cloisters dim,
> And saw nought lovely but the sky and stars.
> But *thou*, my babe! shalt wander like a breeze
> By lakes and sandy shores, beneath the crags
> Of ancient mountain, and beneath the clouds,
> Which image in their bulk both lakes and shores
> And mountain crags: so shalt thou see and hear
> The lovely shapes and sounds intelligible
> Of that eternal language, which thy God
> Utters, who from eternity doth teach
> Himself in all, and all things in himself.

The old Nonconformist belief in portents, signs from God,
is active in this book: Frances's sight of the newts is a special
'favour'. Janet's conclusion, quoting Psalm 121, is hopeful;
Janet knows that the correct reading is interrogative: 'I will
lift up mine eyes unto the hills: from whence cometh my
help?' But only when she sees the sunset does she find any
comfort or meaning in the words. The passage is soaked in
submerged allusions to English Romantic poetry; compare
Percy Bysshe Shelley's 'Ode to the West Wind' (1819), a
prayer for a spiritual and political revolution:

> Thou on whose stream, 'mid the steep sky's commotion
> Loose clouds like earth's decaying leaves are shed,
> Shook from the tangled boughs of Heaven and Ocean,
>
> Angels of rain and lightning: there are spread
> On the blue surface of thine airy surge,
> Like the bright hair uplifted from the head

Of some fierce Maenad, even from the dim verge
Of the horizon to the zenith's height
The locks of the approaching storm. . . .

There is also Samuel Taylor Coleridge's poem 'Christabel' (1816):

The one red leaf, the last of its clan,
That dances as often as dance it can,
Hanging so light, and hanging so high,
On the topmost twig that looks up to the sky.

Landscape and literature are consolatory, though one needs
to be alert to spot Drabble's concealed learning. For example,
Janet, bathing her baby, is reminded that 'she'd read a book
about a woman who'd drowned her baby in the bath after
having a drink too many.' This incident comes from John
Updike's novel, *Rabbit Run* (1960).[8] The wife who drowns the
baby is called Janice.

Janet is afraid of this negative rôle model, and finds more
hope in her acquaintance with Frances, who identifies with
Boadicea, warrior queen of the Iceni, with knives on her
chariot wheels.

Part III takes us through the Valley of the Shadow of Death.
Karel's house looks out over a garden which is in fact a cem-
etery. Karel's wife Joy throws things and provokes Karel into
beating her up. He tells Frances Joy likes it. What are we to
think? Joy is fashionably lesbian and eventually decides to do
the sensible thing and leave. Frances's sister, Alice, who committed suicide, is invoked. Frances's sister-in-law, Natasha,
despite heroically baking her own bread and grinding coffee
beans by hand, is in group therapy. In Part IV Natasha's
student son Stephen, like Empedocles, kills himself—and his
baby. His cremation takes them 'into the red crater, made one
with nature, transformed to black ash'. Lady Ollerenshaw's
demand for more abortion is equated with child sacrifice.
Later, Frances studies child sacrifice among the Phoenicians,
her chosen people. Sir Frank Ollerenshaw's aunt Connie is
found dead in her unelectrified cottage, her stomach full
of cardboard. Frances the archaeologist goes through her
own great-aunt's relics and discovers the secret of Connie's
illegitimate child. Connie, too, had had a married lover, John.
Karel and Frances marry.

99

This novel is as symbolic, even allegorical, as *The Needle's Eye*, but better plotted and written with more control.

As Nora Foster Stovel finely says:

> Frances is free to choose gold or lead, survival or suicide, for both exist as surely as the Pacific, but only a spirit as adventurous as Cortez can discover the golden realm.[10]

Stovel's chapter should be read in full.

Shelley's poem, 'Ozymandias', is invoked. Images of heat and aridity also run through the work. Other critics have found the Demeter-Persephone myth,[11] womb imagery and the insight that Frances is digging into Mother Earth.

In a richly suggestive chapter, Susanna Roxman analyses the images of the novel—the landscape and vegetation which Frances and Karel observe from the car is 'half metallic and half dead'—and notes the integrated use of 'silver birches' in the passage.[12]

Ruminating on the theme of death, she observes that John probably drowned himself, and that this sailor's end is 'a death by water (another instance of Margaret Drabble's association—illicit love, as in George Eliot)'.[13] In her exploration of the earth, Frances the archaeologist literally 'digs' in the soil, and eventually ends up digging her own garden (a cliché here subtly used); her grandparents had tilled the soil for a living. Roxman notes that

> there is earth as minerals, earth as mud or sand or soil, earth as vegetation, and earth as tilled land, giver of food. The earth is moreover a depository of riches, archaeological and geological. . . . We meet one earthquake inspector who claims to be in love with a seismologist. Finally earth is a place of burial . . . a metonymical symbol of death.[14]

Roxman points to the time aspect and to kinship, and reminds us that Drabble's vision of an 'ancient labourer' is compared to Wordsworth's Leech-gatherer,[15] and tells us that Colin Butler regards 'a non-privileged pregnant woman in *The Millstone* as another' such figure.[16] Karel's position as a Jew, historically forbidden to own land, and his specialism as a historian of English eighteenth-century agricultural history are pointed out. The fire symbolism in the novel is finely analysed, and Roxman observes that Janet Bird has characteristics traditionally ascribed to witches.[17] Frances is linked to queens. Roxman concludes in this illuminating section, that Frances, in reclaiming the past, makes it possible to build the future. Roxman's analysis should be read in full.

Interviewed by Olga Kenyon, Drabble said her habit of addressing the reader was

> now called post-modernism, but the Victorians called it the narrator speaking directly to the reader . . . we [assume] that the reader is as intelligent as we are. . . . There's a sort of dialogue going on. The omniscient narrator is disappearing.[18]

Joanne V. Creighton, however, suggests the question is more complicated than that; she argues that Drabble

> creates such a controlling narrative presence in order to undercut its authority and control, to show that indeed 'omniscience has its limits' in the modern world and the modern novel. She has, in effect, turned a nineteenth-century convention into a post-modernist device, establishing the text, at least in part, as a metafiction, a fiction about the writing of fiction.[19]

As Mary Hurley Moran writes: 'Drabble's novels portray a bleak, often menacing universe governed by a harsh supernatural force that allows human beings very little free will.'[20] Drabble admitted to Monica Mannheimer that while Karel and Frances seem to have more 'freedom and spontaneity' than Rose and Simon, this appearance of freedom and happiness 'can only be achieved by a lot of tricks in the plot'.[21] She confessed to me in interview that the character of Frances had been partly engineered to placate the feminists. The book sold well in America but, in Drabble's view, 'for the wrong reasons', because Frances was a strong, active woman. In fact, as we have seen, despite her success, she has the hang-ups of her predecessors.

Ellen Cronan Rose observes, '*The Realms of Gold* is a beautiful novel. But despite its happy ending, it is not, finally, very optimistic about the condition of England and of contemporary society.'[22] Cronan Rose adds, 'Anthea Zeman calls *The Realms of Gold* "a defiantly, blatantly optimistic novel from a professed pessimist".[23] It is an aberration. The age of gold is succeeded by *The Ice Age*.'[24]

In *The Realms of Gold* Frances and Karel, at the end,

are restored to happiness, largely through luck, in a novel about kinship, roots, death and survival of the species. Such harmony as there is in the world comes through love and the vision splendid. They establish, together, a new family when Frances's daughter Daisy marries Karel's son Bob. But there is always strife, as well as love. We get a sly reminder of the political world in the names of Frances's warring Olleren-shaw ancestors: Ted had quarrelled with Enoch, just as Ted Heath, then Conservative Prime Minister, quarrelled with Enoch Powell, whose opinions the moderate Heath found excessively right-wing. *The Ice Age* and *The Middle Ground* are political novels, *The Ice Age* dealing with Britain, *The Middle Ground* with global problems.

NOTES

1. The material was not altogether new: in *The Weather in the Streets* (1936), Rosamond Lehmann, to whom Drabble's work owes much, in style and subject-matter, tells the story of Olivia, mistress to a selfish married man, and her abortion.
2. Olga Kenyon, *Women Writers Talking*, pp. 45–6.
3. Interview with Diana Cooper Clark, reprinted in Ellen Cronan Rose (ed.), *Critical Essays*, p. 27.
4. Interview with Joanne Creighton, reprinted in Dorey Schmidt (ed.), *Margaret Drabble: Golden Realms*, pp. 29–30.
5. Kenyon, p. 34.
6. The distinction between 'organic' and 'inorganic' was important on the Newnham English course. The contrast underpins this novel. At Newnham, moreover, Coleridge's metaphor of organic unity in a work of art was taken extremely seriously. The Leavises, then influential, believed that in the old days there had been 'an organic community'. Frances in the novel recognizes that primitive life was hard and wretched and is grateful for clean sheets.
7. Kenyon, p. 41.
8. Updike, a Lutheran, evinces a metaphysic and a morality which have affinities with Drabble's. Updike's characters inhabit a fallen world.
9. Susanna Roxman points out that Frances is used to excavating tombs; Hugh's house, too, borders on a graveyard. 'Thus at least six cemeteries figure in the narrative, including one glimpse of the future' (*Guilt and Glory*, p. 101). Roxman notes the abundance of 'bones, skulls and teeth'.
10. Nora Foster Stovel, *Margaret Drabble: Symbolic Moralist*, p. 130.

11. Judy Little, 'Humour and the Female Quest: Margaret Drabble's *The Realms of Gold*', *Regionalism and the Female Imagination*, 4, 44–52.
12. Susanna Roxman, *Guilt and Glory*, pp. 188–89.
13. Roxman, p. 189.
14. Roxman, p. 190.
15. Roxman, p. 192.
16. Colin Butler, 'Margaret Drabble: *The Millstone* and Wordsworth', *English Studies: A Journal of English Language and Literature* (1978).
17. Roxman, p. 195.
18. Olga Kenyon, *Women Writers Talking*, pp. 34–5.
19. Joanne V. Creighton, *Margaret Drabble*, p. 83. In 'The Reader and Modern and Post-Modern Fiction', *College Literature* (Fall 1982), Creighton usefully analyses the structure of *The Waterfall*. This essay is reprinted in Ellen Cronan Rose (ed.), *Critical Essays*, p. 117.
20. Mary Hurley Moran, *Margaret Drabble: Existing Within Structures*, p. 18.
21. Drabble's reply to Monica Mannheimer's 'The Search for Identity in Margaret Drabble's *The Needle's Eye*', *Dutch Quarterly Review of Anglo-American Letters*, 5, 1/1976.
22. Ellen Cronan Rose, *Equivocal Figures*, p. 107.
23. Anthea Zeman, *Presumptuous Girls: Women and their world in the Serious Woman's Novel* (London: Weidenfeld, 1977), p. 150.
24. Cronan Rose, *Equivocal Figures*, p. 10.

8

The Ice Age (1977)

Drabble's extra-fictional statements about religious faith are fluctuating and contradictory: she believes that God has special purposes, but is not sure he exists. Yet she believes in revelation, either through Wordsworthian 'spots of time' or from digging into the past, returning to one's origins and finding one's roots. She believes in coincidence and in fate. Though joy may legitimately be snatched from golden moments, the author constantly ponders inequality and injustice and what seem to be undeserved punishments. Like *The Needle's Eye*, *The Ice Age* is about the struggle between God and Mammon, and ends with the search for God and the hope of spiritual renewal. Property developer Anthony, son of the parsonage, returns on the death of his father to the cathedral close where he was reared, and rediscovers the cathedral's values. He has thought the buildings he was responsible for were the 'real world', but in prison in Walachia he plans to write a book about God. Like the cabinet minister evoked in Anton Chekhov's play, *Three Sisters* (Vershinin's speech in Act II), he watches birds from his prison cell and thinks these 'innocent slight spirits' are messengers from God. He becomes interested in that work of stoicism, *The Consolations of Philosophy*, by the Roman Boethius (480–524). Indeed, *The Ice Age* as a whole is a meditation on Boethius.

In the *Consolations*, the author's guardian, Philosophy, discovers that although the author believes God rules the world, Boethius lacks self-knowledge. The second book is about Fortune (and Anthony's career in the novel exemplifies the medieval wheel of Fortune, with its progress from high to low estate). In the third book, Philosophy shows Boethius that true happiness is to be found in God alone, and that real evil does not exist. Book IV asks why, if God is good, do evils exist, and why is virtue often punished and vice rewarded? Philosophy then discusses providence and fate, and shows that every fortune is good. The fifth and last book attempts to reconcile man's free will and God's foreknowledge.

Boethius was well known and popular until the eighteenth century. Among those who consoled themselves by reading him in prison were Giovanni Jacopo Casanova de Seingalt (1725–1798), author of the famous memoirs, and John Horne Tooke (1736–1812), the radical politician and philologist.

Interviewed by Barbara Milton, Drabble said:

> I suppose we just never know that the pattern is. I suppose it is perfectly possible that one will die without knowing what it was all about. But I have this deep faith that it will all be revealed to me one day. One day I shall just see into the heart of the whole thing. A lot of people give up. They realise that there isn't an answer. Maybe that's what will happen to me. Maybe when I'm ten years older I'll decide that I was just deluding myself. But I haven't got to that stage.[1]

In an illuminating discussion, John Hannay relates 'fate' in Drabble's work to three conventional plots: the tragic romance (*The Waterfall*); the return to origin and rediscovery of destiny (*Jerusalem the Golden*, *The Needle's Eye* and *The Realms of Gold*); and the Providential model, in which the guilt of a protagonist is expiated according to divine justice. Oedipus, running to avoid his fate and thereby meeting it, is invoked in *The Waterfall* and in *The Realms of Gold*. Hannay defines a dialectic whereby the text of *The Ice Age* disarms criticism by first claiming that it treats its subject realistically, but then implies that reality follows literary conventions: nature imitates art. (And art imitates nature imitating art: Anthony, recruited as a British spy, reads a spy novel by the master of the genre, John Le Carré.) Hannay's is a useful reading of the sharp, even playful tone with which Drabble confronts personal tragedy (maiming, handicap, bankruptcy, imprisonment) head on. Hannay considers the narrative tone to be 'self-mocking' throughout: 'The word *fate* usually appears in clichéd, pretentious phrases that nonetheless turn out to signal crucial developments of plot or of character.'[2] I would not totally agree; I would describe the tone as one of heroic courage pitted against the ironies and cruelties of life. As in life itself, there are gleams of hilarity among the chaos of apocalypse. Hannay concludes:

> How much Anthony's resurrection has to do with England's remains a critical problem with the book, which indicates a dialectical opposition in the name of realism, to the Providential model. But . . . the misfortunes and setbacks he endures are typical of his generation and are justified in the end by his faith.[3]

(Drabble at the time of writing hardly believed national salvation was possible; her first heroine, Sarah Bennett, did not believe that people can be changed: '. . . they can only be saved or enlightened or renewed, one by one, which is a different thing, and not one that can be effected by legislation.')

Hannay concludes that for Drabble

> Providence remains an eternally receding vision, by definition ungraspable in mundane terms: it is an intertext that the realistic novel can respectfully acknowledge, but must set aside in the end.[4]

Here I take issue: Providence, one might argue, has brought Anthony to repentance. Even Len Wincobank finds charity in his heart for old, mad Callendar, the prisoner who believes (a wonderful touch) that 'something has gone seriously wrong with the laws of chance'.

Drabble herself was uncertain about the ending. In her interview with me, she said:

> I intended to redeem this overwhelming gloom by some kind of vision of Britain rising out of its chains, and in fact, I've used the quotation from Milton about Britain stirring in its chains and rising up. But when I got to the passage, and I knew where it had to come, my characters were sitting in a night club and everything was very bad, and one character, my main character, had to have this vision of Britain, an aerial vision of recovery, and *I couldn't get it*. I couldn't resolve the problem I'd set myself, which was to have some kind of uplift,

optimism, resolution. I think I have finally solved it, but I was stuck with that paralysis for far, far longer than I liked, and I think that was reflecting not art, but life.[5]

Anthony has a vision of a 'semi-precious stone set in a leaden sea, our heritage. . .'. This vision is an ironic counterpoint to the famous words of John of Gaunt in Shakespeare's *Richard II*, where 'this England' is described as a 'precious stone set in a silver sea'. For Alison, England is a 'safe, shabby, mangey old lion now: anyone could tweak her tail.'

The book, now fourteen years old, seems oddly topical in 1991: we still have an oil crisis, economic stagnation, a failed property boom, bankruptcies, financial scandals with ensuing prison sentences, and I.R.A. bombs. The novel is about the condition of England after the oil crisis of 1973, the consequent inflation in property, the 'Winter of Discontent' and the three-day week which nearly paralysed British industry under Ted Heath's Conservative government. Ellen Z. Lambert wrote in 1980 of Drabble that

> her true strength as a writer is a lyric strength: what *happens* in her novels is not really the important thing . . . her reader must be willing to tolerate a good deal of implausibility.[6]

(In *The Ice Age*, what happens is very important, but an unintegrated 'clever bitch, Helen', is introduced merely to observe that hands give away one's age, a mannerism after Virginia Woolf.) Lambert concludes that 'implausible minor characters, implausible plots and (especially) implausible endings' do not 'interfere with the essential pleasure of reading Drabble', which comes from her sense of unexpected hope. Lambert notes that Drabble is praised for writing about 'love, marriage and the bearing of children', yet is also accused of falsifying these spheres.

Contrary to her reputation, Drabble is no analyst of marriage. Marriages in her fiction follow, with minor variations, a stereotyped pattern; characteristically, her leading characters make an eccentric choice of partner from motives of rebellion, and regret it. Crockery-throwing and domestic violence ensue, sex is a chore, but children bring delight as well as anxiety. Emma in *The Garrick Year* commits adultery without enjoying it; Jane in *The Waterfall* and Frances in *The Realms of Gold* get their first orgasms from lovers married to other women. None of the other rocks on which marriages splinter are canvassed: there are no gamblers; wives are not much distressed by their husbands' adulteries, as they are busy committing adultery themselves; the only alcoholic is Frances's brother Hugh; until *The Ice Age* money worries are conspicuous by their absence. After *The Needle's Eye*, characters tend to be divorced and to stay that way. Anthony has married a feather-headed bumbler, who supplies comic relief; Alison has married a feckless actor. After the birth of her spastic daughter, Alison gives up her own stage career and becomes a full-time charity worker. She must have an (unexplained) private income, for she can afford to send her daughter to an expensive private school. Alison and Anthony, though both divorced, are, like Rose and Simon in *The Needle's Eye*, prevented from marrying by circumstances.

The Ice Age marks out fresh ground; it has weight and substance. The plotting is masterly, minor characters both integrated and plausible, with the uncomfortable exception of the saintly Kitty, a Jewish lady so kind-hearted that she can plead for both Zionists and Palestinians and celebrate Christian as well as Jewish festivals. Kitty is a grotesque, with her dyed red hair, ill-applied make-up and old fur coats; we feel the character is being patronized by the author, falling over backwards not to be racist. However, in general the writing is subtle and satisfying and the morality sound, if traditional and unsurprising. Once again, Drabble evades political commitment and turns to spiritual values. Anthony has been 'seduced and corrupted'; Alison, Anthony's mistress, Len Wincobank and Len's mistress, Maureen Kirby, have all been 'corrupted'; Len has a 'black heart'. Anthony neither likes nor trusts his 'friend' and partner, Giles. They have all relied on 'stimulants' and 'condiments' in their temporary days of affluence, which in various ways they live to repent at leisure.

Michael F. Harper acutely notes that Drabble's novels stretch 'with difficulty from lower-middle to upper-middle class but [are] unable to comprehend radically different contexts'.[7] Drabble told Nancy Poland in 1975:

> There must be a lot of people like me. A lot of people have got exactly the same worries and problems. In a way, if you

look at it, I am a very ordinary person. I've got three children; I sort of scrub my floors. I worry about whether I'm using my education; I worry about India and Africa and Vietnam. So does everybody. No, I'm not pretending that everybody's a Cambridge graduate, but I do assert quite strongly that my daily life is very like most people's.[8]

This may have been 'sort of' true in 1975; today Drabble is a superstar. Her appropriation of Oxbridge and Hampstead as fictional material have made it difficult for others with similar experiences to use them in writing without being accused of plagiarism. Interviewed by Diana Cooper-Clark, Drabble criticized Jane Austen:

. . . she ought to have had a slightly greater awareness of what was going on in the rest of England. It's got nothing to do with range, it has to do with social conscience, which George Eliot had and which gave the books a greater breadth. Now Mrs. Gaskell had a very great social conscience, and although her books are narrow in a way and they're women's books in a way (she wrote about motherhood extremely well), she had this passionate concern for the unfortunate, which is something that I'm very much drawn to in fiction and in life. I think that novels that concentrate on a very small section of society, however brilliantly, like Evelyn Waugh for example, are missing out too much to be truly great.[9]

Yet the real empathy in *The Ice Age* is for the middle-class characters: Len and Maureen are seen from the outside, like creatures from another planet, though their greed is excused by their original poverty. The book's message is the superiority of culture (which embodies spiritual values) to commerce. Culture is only safe in the hands of the children of the professional middle class, like Anthony, who strays but is gathered, after tribulation, back into the fold. Like a Victorian hero, he is purified by suffering. 'Upstarts' (her word) like Mike Morgan, who makes a living as a stand-up comic who abuses his audiences, are not to be trusted. Mike Morgan made his way to Oxford, but he is a miner's son and does not have the hereditary advantages and responsibilities that devolve on Anthony. Anthony has been 'vaguely and carelessly progress-ive', while living the life of a capitalist; Alison has no political creed, but believes (like her author) in the Health Service and the Social Services (threatened, since the time the novel was written, by the Conservative government's actions). The upper classes, represented by Giles and his awful girlfriend, Pamela, who neglects her dogs, are self-seeking and unreliable. The working-class characters Drabble manages best are those who have struggled up through grammar school and university to the professions, like Simon Camish. (An exception, admittedly, is the fine short story, 'The Spoils of War'.) Drabble would probably be surprised that readers should find her work conservative, in the manner of Jane Austen, but so were her models, Dickens, Disraeli, Mrs. Gaskell, George Eliot and even Charles Kingsley (1819–75). The socialist novelists, such as Robert Tressell (1870–1911) have had no influence on Drabble's work. Lynn Veach Sadler suggests that 'Drabble suggests that the élite have gotten her country nowhere—but neither have those who have imbibed America's entrepreneurial spirit.'[10] She writes that Drabble's picture of the 'huge icy fist . . . squeezing and chilling the people of Britain . . . fixing them . . . like fish in a frozen river' is far from the redeemed vision of 'eighteenth-century cows munching along in their "golden age" near Aunt Con's grave in *The Realms of Gold*'.[11] Sadler thinks Drabble is at fault to write that Alison, unlike England, will never recover: 'The ringing question comes back from us—"Whyever not?" Her smug dismissal of Alison is a weakness.'[12]

Sadler frequently shows impatience with Drabble: here she shows insensitivity, forgetting that Alison's life is forever ruined not by the loss of her lover and the incarceration of her daughter Jane, but by the responsibility for Jane's sister Molly, the daughter with cerebral palsy. The author pleads eloquently against government neglect of the handicapped, in the omniscient narrator's voice.

Ellen Cronan Rose observes that

> the central male enterprise in *The Ice Age* is the assertion of the superiority of culture over nature. In *The Realms of Gold* this attitude was indicted as leading to ecological disaster. . . .[13]

Drabble has always been concerned with the place of the arts in life. This novel asks whether traditional culture is in retreat? The few pages on Linton Hancox, classicist and former poet, are among the most eloquent she has written. A former golden boy with curly hair, Linton is now fat and grey (Bacchus, it is implied, has become Silenus). Formerly progressive, Linton is now a soured reactionary. His wife is unfaithful and he is having an affair in revenge and to spite the woman's husband. (Anthony and Len, for different reasons, are reduced to impotence, literal and symbolic.) Anthony wonders who, in a recession, can afford the luxury of Greek?

Linton ponders the status of his subject in elegiac terms:

> He thought of Antigone, descending into her living tomb, her bridal bower. The three fates.
> On her the grey fates laid hard hands.
> Choose death, before it chooses you. They were all dead, all the young men and maidens, Antigone, Hector, Penelope, Cressida, Achilles, Orestes, Clytemnestra. The faithful and the faithless, all dead. And what difference did it make? . . . A scholastic stronghold, standing out against the barbarians, with the living flame within? Or an empty shrine, a pillaged tomb? . . . The Muse was silent. . . . Was she dead therefore, or dead to him alone? Would she ride back in triumph over the Eastern plains, clanking with armour, ferocious reborn matriarch, drinking blood?
> There is no blood left in me, thought Linton Hancox. I am a dry husk, dry as parchment. There is no blood in my veins, but some strange woody sap. Xylem or phloem. A protective spirit has mercifully turned me into a tree, to spare me the rape of the mind.

This last paragraph is about the opposition of nature and culture: in classical mythology, Daphne was turned into a laurel bush by Zeus to avoid rape by the god Apollo. Daphne escaped culture and reverted to nature, imaged in the novel by a stoat Linton sees in his car headlights, crossing his path. The spirit of Antigone is invoked later when Anthony makes his useless, but admirable, self-sacrifice, so that Jane can get away from Walachia. In fact, Walachia is not a country, but an old province of Romania. Wordsworth's sonnet, 'June 1820', alludes to Walachia as 'groves—from England far away—/ Groves that inspire the Nightingale to trill'. The sonnet is patriotic, as Drabble is patriotic; it extols British songbirds, standing for British poets, and explicitly James

Thomson (1700–48) as at least the equals of foreign competitors. Drabble now asks, how are the arts and culture, which embody spiritual values, doing in England now?

Drabble's epigraphs come from Milton's cry for freedom and progress, *Areopagitica* (1644), and Wordsworth's call to the spirit of Milton: 'Milton, thou should'st be living at this hour:/ England hath need of thee. . . .'

Drabble admitted that the novel was about economic depression. 'But I don't want Americans to read *The Ice Age* as a portrait of England going down the drain.'[14] In her interview with me, Drabble said:

> I'm very worried that this book will be seen as an account of economic collapse and despair and dismalness, and I think it's interesting that my American publisher rang me up from New York and said, 'I've just finished your book, what a terrifying experience'; whereas my English publisher rang me up and said, 'What a very funny book.'

Joanne V. Creighton relates the novel to Angus Wilson's *No Laughing Matter* (1967), John Fowles's *Daniel Martin* (1977) and, especially, Malcolm Bradbury's *The History Man* (1975): 'Depicting the collapse of humanistic values in a determining world, these two novels are similar in their wry and detached portrait of exemplary men of the age.'[15]

Newspaper critics complained that *The Ice Age* was too full of sensational and improbable incidents, such as the terrorist bomb in the restaurant where Max and Kitty are celebrating their Ruby Wedding. Max is killed and Kitty loses a foot. Any reader of newspapers knows that terrorist bombs are an everyday occurrence in Britain, killing and injuring innocent people. Drabble's fictional range has widened from young women facing their destinies to philosophical evaluation of destiny itself. As Mary Hurley Moran points out, newspapers occupy a special place in Drabble's work: newspapers are the individual's link with the wider public world, and reading them is a duty.[16] We remember that Rose Vertue Vassiliou felt guilty when the Welfare Officer called and found her reading the *Guardian* instead of washing the floor.

Drabble read Oliver Marriott's *The Property Boom* as research for this novel and records that she travelled around England with a 'property speculator in his golden Rolls-Royce which was all he had left from his money—he had lost the lot—and we looked at the buildings that he had created'.[17] In the same book, she comments:

> By this time I was very conscious of symbolism and a lot of it takes place in prison. There are a lot of prisons in the book. Three characters are in real prisons and there are many spiritual imprisonments as well within the book.[18]

This is true: the obvious comparison is with Dickens's *Little Dorrit* (1855–57), a novel about the psychology of confinement and the prison of the self. *The Ice Age* is responsible for Drabble's latter-day reputation as a Dickensian novelist, because of its picture of London squalor and high finance. However, the Dickensian and Shakespearean echoes go back at least to *The Needle's Eye*; Dickens and Shakespeare inform the British literary imagination.

Prisons are adumbrated throughout the text: we learn that Anthony once locked himself into a lavatory, and contemplated hanging himself with his belt. As the novel opens, Anthony is virtually imprisoned. His health deprives him of nicotine, alcohol and sexual activity. He may be bankrupt—but is not certain. He is isolated. The initial irony is that the property developer, who has evicted old ladies from their terrace homes in city centres and demolished their corner shops, lives in a grand country mansion, High Rook House (for Anthony, along with other property developers, has 'rooked' the nation). He ends up in a real prison, in the fictional iron curtain country of Walachia.

Drabble supplies, hardly disturbing the smooth flow of her narrative, a potted history of the Balkans through Anthony's struggle to remember: the fall of Constantinople, Serbian independence, the war with Turkey, right up to the Warsaw Pact. 'Both Albania and Walachia had subsequently withdrawn from the Warsaw Pact, though for different ideological reasons. When? He could not remember. Why? He had never known.' The Iron Curtain country is invoked as a contrast to the affluence of Britain, even a Britain in decline; Alison is glad to get back to her creature comforts.

Drabble recognizes that to those of her and my generation, brought up during the war,

affluence had always been an unreal delusion . . . now, with
a sense of virtue, they could go round switching off fires and
lowering the power of electric light bulbs, bathing in water
three inches deep, using up old crusts and thinning sauces in
the bottoms of old bottles with vinegar . . . according to their
enemies, their philosophy was: *it is wrong to enjoy oneself, it is
right to sit in the cold by a candle end.* But they, in fact, enjoyed
sitting by a candle end.

This paragraph is characteristic Drabble: accurate sociology
and psychology, it makes us laugh. Yet the book's tendency
as a whole is not to mock, but to vindicate, asceticism. Alison
Murray is irritated by the privations of life in Iron Curtain
Walachia, but Anthony loses the whole world there and gains
his own soul.

Then there are 'the war babies . . . astonished at their own
purchasing power each time they bought a pound of bananas
or a small pot of double cream', while

odd new groups on the far left hoped that each rise in the bank
rate and each strike in a car factory heralded the final collapse
of capitalism. Sociologists expressed approval of the rate of
social change. . . . Out of this, some sincerely believed, would
rise a new order, of selfless, social, greedless beings. . . . There
were also the real poor: the old, the unemployed, the undesir-
able immigrants. . . . Let us not think of them. Their rewards
will be in heaven. . . . Finally, there was the small communion
of saints, who truly hoped that from this crisis would come a
better sharing among the nations of the earth: who truly in
their hearts applauded the rise in price of raw materials from
the poorer countries of the earth: who thought of the poor,
and of themselves rarely, and included themselves among the
rich, which most of them, by Western European standards,
were not.

'Could even God's love,' asks the narrator, 'suffice this
multitude? . . . This is the state of the nation.'

We return to Anthony, who remembers the Diggers, who
had dug up Richmond Hill in an attempt at primitive com-
munism, public ownership of land, and been ruthlessly suppressed by Oliver Cromwell. Cromwell ruled England for
eleven years after 1649, when he and the other Parliamen-
tarians cut off the head of King Charles I. But the Diggers
were too radical even for Oliver the regicide. Anthony thinks

of the enclosure of common lands, which led to poor folk losing their right to graze animals. Anthony does not make the connexion between wholesale demolition in order to build new office blocks, causing old ladies like Maureen Kirby's Aunt Evie to be evicted, and the Enclosure Acts which led to 'more efficient' farming by landowners, but the alert reader does. Anthony is not surprised 'that neither political party had a coherent housing policy. Homes not offices, declared placards all over London, accusing property developers like Anthony Keating of the wrong priorities.'

Although Drabble does not say so, the previous Labour government in the late 1960s had demolished homes to build hotels in order to accommodate visitors to London. This policy pushed people farther out into the suburbs, forcing them to commute, thus adding to traffic congestion, and leading to an escalation in house prices. Anthony wonders whether London 'is going the way of New York—garbage-strewn, transport-choked, dirty'.

A mouse runs over Anthony's hearth rug in his Yorkshire retreat, 'not unlike a prison', as he reflects that it 'is not every clergyman's son who has an opportunity to visit a good friend in jail'.

The property boom is equated with a gamble: 'The flow had ceased to flow: the ball had stopped rolling: the game of musical chairs was over. *Rien ne va plus*, the croupier had shouted. . . .'

The key scene in the novel is Anthony's return to his native cathedral city. As he approaches,

> The sky was full of a peculiar radiance: the sun was shining from behind banked clouds, glancing downwards in those strange religious rays beloved of landscape painters, and lighting the cathedral's roof and spire with a golden light. It was a classic scene, and had, indeed, in such a light, been much painted, by Turner, by Girtin, by Prout. . . . Under this shadow had Anthony Keating been reared, in the circumference of these rays. Well, he had got out. Had built his own cathedrals, bought his own close.

Anthony has been reared, literally, in the 'shadow' of the cathedral, and here the rays of sunshine, traditional image of God's influence, are invoked as an image of the eternal;

art and religion are eternal verities. Anthony's mother has a real silver teapot, but like Aunt Evie she is threatened with homelessness when her husband dies; her elegant home is a kind of tied cottage. In the cathedral, which has always been 'too much for him', Anthony finds it impossible not to be moved by what he still thinks of as 'ancient illusion'. For him, 'Len Wincobank, Harry Hyams, Richard Seifert . . . were the modern builders. And Centre Point stood as empty as Crawford Cathedral, an anachronism before it had even been occupied.'

(Richard Seifert and Harry Hyams are real people; Hyams's Centre Point is a tall, empty office block at the junction of London's Charing Cross Road and Tottenham Court Road, a skyscraper.)

Anthony reflects that whereas his own commercial cathedral, Imperial House, had been built in two years, the cathedral had taken longer. 'The craftsmen of Crawford had been secure for many decades in their work.' At this stage, Anthony still has dreams of making his fortune. On the train, 'he opened his daily paper and read about North Sea Oil, the black miracle, the *Deus Ex Machina*', and he wonders whether Britain might be saved at the last hour. Drabble's books are always 'about salvation' and 'saved' carries its full equivocal weight. Anthony wonders whether he lives in 'A senile Britain, casting out its ghosts. Or a Go Ahead Britain, with oil-rig men toasting their mistresses in champagne in the pubs of Aberdeen.'

Anthony returns, recklessly, to smoking and heavy drinking then releases himself from the triple partnership. There is a brief idyll with Alison. Anthony thinks that 'peace is so expensive, love is fitful, destruction so relentless. A thrush sang in the apple tree in the garden, despite this.'

And that thrush is a familiar symbol of hope, ever since Thomas Hardy's in his poem, 'The Darkling Thrush':

> So little cause for carollings
>   Of such ecstatic sound
> Was written on terrestrial things
>   Afar or nigh around,
> That I could think there trembled through
>   His happy goodnight air

116

Some blessed hope, whereof he knew
And I was unaware.

Anthony is guilty of *hubris*, the pride which is punished by the gods in Greek tragedy. He thinks he has 'tackled the modern capitalist economy. He was a modern man, an operator, at one with the spirit of the age.' But his wife, though not particularly intelligent, suspects that Anthony's friends and colleagues are 'all crooks'; she is

> not the only person to suspect that Anthony's sense of empire was illusory. Alison Murray also suspected it, but unlike Babs, she had a vested interest in believing it to be real. If Anthony became a rich man, Babs would lose him and Alison would get him.

The night before he leaves for Walachia to collect Alison's daughter Jane, released from prison, Anthony wonders what social change in Britain has been worth; they had all known the past was dead, that it was time for a New Age.

> But nothing had arisen to fill the gap. . . . He and his clever friends . . . had thrown out the mahogany and bought cheap stripped pine, they had slept with one another's wives and divorced their own, they had sent their children to state schools, they had acquired indeterminate accents, they had made friends from unthinkable quarters, they had encouraged upstarts like Mike Morgan, they had worn themselves out and contorted themselves trying to understand a new system, a new egalitarian culture, the new illiterate visual television age. . . . They had learned, academics, teachers, and parents alike, to condemn the examinations that had elevated them and brought them security. . . . Nothing had changed. Where was the new bright classless enterprising future of Great Britain? In jail with Len Wincobank, mortgaged to the hilt with North Sea Oil.

This passage is a severe indictment of the fashionable woolly pseudo-socialism of the '60s and '70s; it is also a statement of spiritual crisis. Anthony recognizes that he belongs to the world that has gone,

> reared in the shelter of a cathedral built to a faith that I have sometimes wished I could share, educated in ideals of public service which I have sometimes wished I could fulfil, a child

of a lost empire, disinherited, gambler, drinker, hypocrite: and who am I to resist an appeal to a chivalric spirit that was condemned as archaic by Cervantes?

He decides to be a weed on the tide of history. Approaching the prison, he suddenly thinks, 'I do not know how a man can do without God . . . he stopped in the roadway, like Paul on the way to Damascus.'

(Rose, in *The Needle's Eye*, describes a religious revelation in these terms, of heavenly light.) The allusion is to the conversion of St. Paul, formerly a persecutor of Christians, and called Saul:

And Saul, yet breathing out threatenings and slaughter against the disciples of the Lord, went unto the high priest. . . .

And as he journeyed, he came near Damascus: and suddenly there shined round about him a light from heaven.

And he fell to the earth, and heard a voice saying unto him, Saul, Saul, why persecutest thou me?

And he said, Who art thou, Lord? And the Lord said, I am Jesus whom thou persecutest: it is hard for thee to kick against the pricks.

And he, trembling and astonished said, Lord, what wilt thou have me to do, And the Lord said unto him, Arise, and go into the city, and it shall be told thee what thou must do.

This comes from the New Testament, Acts of the Apostles, 9: 1–6. The 'road to Damascus' and its heavenly light are recognized symbols for enlightenment and change of heart. The most famous pictorial representation is by Caravaggio (1573–1610), now hanging in the church of Santa Maria del Popolo, in Rome. This painting shows a stunned St. Paul fallen off his horse.

In theological terms, prevenient grace is working in Anthony: he is not yet consciously seeking God, but God is seeking him.

The Macbeth echoes continue. Anthony thinks of sleeping with Jane to cheer her up: 'had she not so, in her loss of adolescent weight, resembled Alison, he would have done it', which recalls Lady Macbeth's revulsion against murdering Duncan, who resembled her father as he slept; the council's decision to rehouse Maureen's Aunt Evie robs her of 'the

rewards of old age—honour, love, civility, streets of friends'.
Macbeth, doomed, recognizes that

> that which should accompany old age,
> As honour, love obedience, troops of friends,
> I must not look to have.

The sausages Anthony cooks for supper recognize only two
stages, the 'raw and the burned'. This is an allusion to the
theory of Claude Lévi-Strauss, *Le Cru et le Cuit*. Drabble rec-
ommended to me his *Tristes Tropiques*, when I saw her wear-
ing a sweatshirt labelled 'Lévi-Strauss'. I asked her if she were
a convert to structuralism. 'They're the people who make the
jeans', she replied, laughing, but the conversation led us to
the French author.

In this book, the evaluation of characters by other characters is handled with considerable subtlety. Alison, quarrelling
with Jane, her resentful daughter, tells her she is mean and
selfish. From one point of view, Alison is justified; yet from
Jane's, the way most of her mother's attention goes to Molly
is a grievance. In any family where there is a handicapped
child, that child absorbs more than its fair share of attention,
and the other children necessarily suffer. Anthony later
recognizes that though Jane is a soured and unpleasant
girl, she has her reasons. Jane thinks of her mother, in her
fur coat, with an 'anti-conservationist' bag (of real leather?
crocodile, perhaps?), as 'gruesome'.

There are hints, though, that Alison and Anthony, middle-
aged lovers, have a touch of Antony and Cleopatra, some
magnificence. A property magnate, like a great ruler, controls
the lives of lesser people. Anthony thinks: 'They have con-
spired behind my back, while I was away. Like Caesar and
Lepidus, while Antony was lolling about with Cleopatra. A
triumvirate cannot work.'

The text is a palimpsest of semi-buried allusion: 'The dark
satanic smoke had gone forever, and Sheffield lay purified
by the apocalyptic flames of a new Jerusalem.' Here we have
Blake's puzzling, but powerful, poem, 'Jerusalem', with its
references to 'dark Satanic mills'. Generally, the 'mills' are
taken to represent Newtonian science, but in the popular
imagination (and 'Jerusalem' is a popular hymn in Britain,

always sung at Women's Institute meetings), they are taken to mean textile factories. And what weight are we to give Derek and Maureen's vision of 'the new Jerusalem'? Derek is an architect, Maureen the former mistress of a property developer. Drabble admires some modern architecture: she has mentioned in conversation that she admired the new tower blocks in Sheffield. But recently, unsatisfactory as homes, they were demolished. In her biography of Arnold Bennett, Drabble writes that she had based *Jerusalem the Golden* on her childhood memories of Sheffield.

> I wrote the book from memory, and then decided I'd better go back and check up that I'd remembered right, so I went up for a night, arriving after dark and staying at the Station Hotel. In the morning I was expecting to look out of the window and see those soul-destroying grim industrial perspectives, but in fact I looked out, the sun was shining, the hillsides were glittering, green fields fringed the horizon, it was all bright and sparkling and beautiful. I felt as though I had maligned the place completely in my memory. After the flat dull overbuilt sprawl of London, it was Sheffield that looked like Jerusalem. Of course, clean air may have had something to do with this impression. Sheffield is a different city now, since the Clean Air Act of 1956: the creation of Smoke Control areas, in 1959 and 1972, has transformed its views and its atmosphere. A similar change has of course overtaken Stoke-on-Trent: Burslem no longer appears from the heights of Sneyd Green to lie 'in a heavy pall of smoke', as Sheffield used to lie in my memories of the 1940s and 1950s, when one returned to it from the hillsides of Derbyshire. (p. 5)

Drabble adds that her own view of Sheffield is 'somewhat constrained'.

This optimistic paragraph was published, however, in 1974, before we realized that the Clean Air act, enforcing tall chimneys, resulted in a boomerang effect: we got rid of smoke at ground level, but by sending the smoke higher into the atmosphere, we induced acid rain. But on balance, one feels that although Drabble is not on the side of the property developers, she shares something of Derek's and Maureen's pleasure in the new Jerusalem of cleaned up northern industrial towns (Northam, the industrial city which recurs in Drabble's fiction, is to be equated with Sheffield.)

But Alison's vision of 'the promised land' is merely the other side of a road clogged with traffic, where an isolated church 'reared up, abandoned, a strange relic, a survivor from another age . . . a pointing finger of ignored reproach'.

There are touches of surreal poetry in the writing: the red empty seats are the 'toothless gums of the theatre' (this is no mere conceit, but is linked with the image of the 'mangey lion' England has become); theatrical art has degenerated into foul-mouthed abuse. Mike Morgan is as guilty of *'trahison des clercs'* as Anthony, with perhaps more excuse. He has a 'white rat-clown face, impassive, cold disdainful'. He tells 'black jokes about blacks, queer jokes about queers. Irish jokes about the Irish, Arab jokes about the Arabs', then mocks his audience for laughing. Mike belongs to what is popularly called the 'loony left', apparently; his act includes quotations from Proudhon, alluding to the famous dictum, 'Property is theft', Locke, Hobbes, Marx, 'Engels on the Origin of the Family and Private Property'. These are 'frenzied outpourings', which show 'perfect control of the audience, such timing of hostilities'. Anthony is impressed, though he ought not to be. Mike accuses Anthony and Giles of being exploiters, while he 'works for his living'. Mike is summed up for us by the author, through Anthony's speculative perceptions, as 'a solitary sadist with strong homosexual tendencies, probably unable to satisfy himself because of a mixture of narcissicism and puritanism'. Anthony 'knew, in the silence, that Mike had worked in a brothel, that he had not been employing a figure of speech'. The silence is broken by the sound of a gunshot in the street, which nobody recognizes for what it is.

Yet art does survive: in a Walachian museum, Alison finds

> a wreath, shimmering and quivering, golden, perfect, light, bright, insubstantial. . . . It was made of laurel twigs, with thin beaten leaves; one could see the delicate markings of the twig. The leaves shivered in the artificial light. . . . Hanging from the twigs, on neat little golden loops, were golden berries. . . . The wreath must surely have been a queen's possession. How on earth has it survived burial?

Drabble visited the exhibition of treasures from Bulgaria at the British Museum in the mid-'70s, where a wreath exactly

121

as described was on show. The sight sets off meditations about gold, the gold standard, wealth. Alison, who has played princesses as an actress, had 'turned from gold, and chosen the leaden casket' in abandoning her career to care for Molly. This is an allusion to Shakespeare's play, *The Merchant of Venice*.

Alison has put duty to Molly before the egotism of performing as pretended royalty. Bassanio in Shakespeare's play has the sense to choose the leaden casket, and is rewarded by Portia and her wealth. But although Alison has chosen Anthony, who seems likely to create wealth, she gets no rewards. Alison and her daughter Molly endure undeserved misfortune. Molly's plight is tragic and irreversible, like Kitty's loss of a foot. That is why Alison can never recover. Yet despite the prevalence of disasters, this *is* a funny book: Tim the fantasist, an out-of-work actor who joins Anthony as general cook-handyman, for instance. In *The Needle's Eye*, some of the epic similes and metaphors strike the reader as strained; but in this book one reads every sentence, every paragraph, with fascinated admiration, so meaty and beautifully crafted is the writing.

The prose is resonant and suggestive: 'Anthony's book is not very well written because he is not a very good writer. But he writes for himself. He has lost interest in any market.'

On the primary level, this means he is not interested in publication. It means, on a deeper level, that Anthony has purged himself of his interest in market economics. 'The absence of drink, sex, warmth and human affection have concentrated his mind wonderfully.' This alludes to the famous saying of Dr. Samuel Johnson (1709–84) that when a man knows he is to be hanged in a fortnight 'it concentrates his mind wonderfully'.

Olga Kenyon observes:

> In *The Ice Age* Drabble develops the social analysis, within a more complex construction which includes a love-story, imprisonment and a final clever twist. But the symbols reveal more than the plot: they are what [Ellen] Moers would term 'feminine' as they represent rounded landscapes, gardening and small birds.

She quotes Drabble in interview, 25 January 1985:

I knew half-way through that I needed a bird at the end to resolve that particular shape. It begins with a pheasant, a large artificially-preserved bird, dying of a heart-attack; this is a symbol of the death of the old culture. *The Ice Age* ends with a little rare bird that he sees while in prison in the Balkans. It symbolises the human spirit fluttering for ever in its rare and special way.[19]

The Ice Age also embodies a semi-private symbol: one of the businesses Anthony's activities have destroyed is a sweet factory. Anthony and Giles take over its name, and call themselves the Imperial Delight Property Company. (They have delighted in the new imperial rôle, demolishing to create new kingdoms.) The sweet factory, symbolizing a constant source of simple pleasure, is to be found in *The Needle's Eye*:

. . . full of all the penny and halfpenny sweets, liquor-ice bootlaces, penny chews, gob stoppers, humbugs, toffee strips—that ignorant adults, who no longer frequent such shops believe in their arrogant adulthood to have vanished from the face of the earth. But the sweets are still there.

Drabble's paternal grandparents owned a sweet factory and its mythology is potent within the family: see the short story, 'Sugar', in *Sugar and Other Stories* (1987) by A. S. Byatt. These few examples serve to demonstrate the poetic coherence of this distinguished novel. In the religious tradition, it looks unflinchingly at the terrible world we live in, but never loses sight of hope. Like that of Dickens before her, Drabble's social realism is deeply romantic. Like Dickens and the Romantic poets, who believed in the imagination and the holiness of the heart's affections, she believes in the continuing energy of the spirit.

NOTES

1. Barbara Milton, 'Margaret Drabble: The Art of Fiction', *Paris Review*, 20, 74 (1978), 65.
2. John Hannay, *The Intertextuality of Fate: A Study of Margaret Drabble*, p. 84.
3. Hannay, p. 90.

4. Hannay, p. 98.
5. Nora Foster Stovel discusses the Dantean vision as part of a literary tradition in 'The Aerial View of Modern Britain: The Airplane as a Vehicle for Idealism and Satire', *Ariel*, 15 (Summer 1984), 17–33.
6. Ellen Z. Lambert, 'Margaret Drabble and the Sense of Possibility', *University of Toronto Quarterly*, 49, No. 3 (Spring 1980), 228–51. Reprinted in Ellen Cronan Rose (ed.), *Critical Essays*, p. 31.
7. Michael F. Harper, 'Margaret Drabble and the Resurrection of the English Novel', *Contemporary Literature*, 23, No. 2 (Spring 1982), 145–68. Reprinted in Ellen Cronan Rose (ed.), *Critical Essays*, p. 69.
8. Interview with Nancy Poland, 'Margaret Drabble: "There must be a lot of people like me"', *Midwest Quarterly*, 16 (Spring 1975), 225–67.
9. Interview with Diana Cooper-Clark, *Atlantic Monthly*, 246, No. 5 (November 1980), 69–75. Reprinted in Ellen Cronan Rose, *Critical Essays*, p. 23.
10. Lynn Veach Sadler, *Margaret Drabble*, p. 101.
11. Sadler, p. 106.
12. Sadler, p. 114.
13. Ellen Cronan Rose, *Equivocal Figures*, p. 111.
14. Interview with Mel Gussow, 'Margaret Drabble: A Double Life', *New York Times Book Review*, 9 October 1977.
15. Joanne V. Creighton, *Margaret Drabble*, p. 92.
16. Mary Hurley Moran, *Margaret Drabble: Existing within Structures*, pp. 20–1.
17. Margaret Drabble, *The Tradition of Women's Fiction: Lectures in Japan*, ed. Yukako Suga (Tokyo: Oxford University Press, 1982), p. 89.
18. Ibid., p. 90.
19. Olga Kenyon, *Women Novelists Today*, p. 96.

9

The Middle Ground (1980)

Kate Armstrong, journalist heroine of *The Middle Ground*, is almost a parody of Drabble woman: middle-aged, divorced, an adoring mother, a successful newspaper writer on women's issues, she invites comparison with the author (whom, physically, she even resembles). The picture of marriage is unprecedentedly savage (Stuart, the ex-husband, is not only an unsuccessful painter, but sexually feeble as well, though he has given Kate three children). Kate returns to her origins, only to discover not healing self-knowledge but disillusion: 'I should never have looked, I should never have looked, I should never have looked.' The novel begins and ends with shared meals, and there are various allusions to Virginia Woolf's *Mrs. Dalloway*, which Kate's daughter Ruth is 'doing for A level'. Here, though, Drabble woman is split into Kate, with working-class origins, and her social worker friend Evelyn, who comes from a refined Quaker family, like Drabble herself. Evelyn's husband Ted is Kate's lover, a tangle reminiscent of the set-up in *The Waterfall*. Lynn Veach Sadler finds Evelyn 'more complicated and more sympathetic than Kate. . . . [Evelyn] almost upstages her.'[1] This is because Evelyn is a social type Drabble understands and Kate is outside her range, though Kate's meteoric rise from secretary to columnist is not improbable. Kate's 'crash course' in shorthand and typing, however, is unlikely: in the 1950s such courses were expensive and socially exclusive; girls like Kate were left to struggle at evening classes.

Susanna Roxman says rising by the combination of professional career and marriage, like Kate, is

> typical of men rather than women; the more or less successful females—such as Sarah in *A Summer Birdcage*, Rosamund in

The Millstone, Frances in *The Realms of Gold*—normally do it more on their own, by way of a university education, but also with the support of a solid middle-class upbringing. . . . As in *The Realms of Gold*, place is made to stand for class.[2]

A novel that purports to be about class ought at least to get it right. But Drabble's airy ignorance of working-class life and conditions is a blot on the book. Kate's father is a sewage worker, her mother an agoraphobic.

> The children lived precariously, nervously, subject to teasing, mockery, contempt, outcasts in their own community. It was not, Kate recalls, a very pleasant community anyway, and her mother may have had good reasons for spurning it, but that did not make life any more agreeable. Kate has said several times that she can imagine no way of life more cramping, painful and pointless than the life of the lower-middle-class family aspiring to be better than it is.

This is well said, but we get no more of this promising scenario, rich in tragi-comic potential. Kate's father is a union activist, and

> His speech at his retirement, during the strike of 1970, was a fine piece of oratory, invoking the great pioneering names of Chadwick and Bazalgette, Simon, Godwin and Snow, conjuring up the Dickensian horrors of the polluted Thames, nostalgically recalling the heroism of the three flashers lost during the great flood of 1953.

But we get none of what Mr. and Mrs. Fletcher actually say, apart from one brief outburst from him; Drabble cannot do it, because she has never heard these voices. Kate fails her eleven-plus and goes to a secondary modern school in 1948. Drabble has clearly never been in a secondary modern school in her life: the headmistress has a cut-glass accent and wears tailored tweeds and well-polished brogues. Secondary modern school heads at that time had regional accents and were unlikely to intimidate pupils by 'cultured middle class tones'. 'The academic standards were not high; the brighter girls were steered towards jobs as secretaries and bank clerks and nursery nurses.' Kate leaves, having 'picked up one or two O levels with not very good grades'. O levels had been going for just two years in 1953, when Kate was 16, but she would not have taken them. In secondary modern schools at the time, all pupils left at 15 without any qualifications to work in factories or shops. The only bit Drabble gets right is that Kate does not know French or any other foreign language. The secretaries and bank clerks and nursery nurses came from grammar schools. In the '50s, only 4 per cent of British youngsters went to university at all, and most of that 4 per cent came not from grammar schools, but independent schools like Drabble's own. Kate fronts a TV programme about her former schoolmates, and this section too is embarrassing. Marylou, who has become a film star, and her contemporaries, Edie, Dora, Sharon, Marlene, Jayne and Denise, are cardboard cut-outs: the patronizing sympathy is pure plastic. Their ghastly homes are fastidiously described:

> . . . flowered carpets, best tea-sets, an ingenious variety of draped lace curtains, Spanish-style vinyl tiles, wall clocks rayed like the sun in never-dying deco, china Siamese cats and pigs and dogs, Toby jugs, glass fish, plastic rabbits, rubbery trolls, outsize turquoise teddies, plastic daffodils, plastic palm trees, fake fur rugs bristling with spidery white acrylic electric light, all the wonderful eclectic bad taste of the English, the brave new world of synthesis.

As Susanna Roxman says:

> Marylou's loneliness is perhaps the price Marylou has to pay for being a freak. The actress may even be authorially punished for not having accepted her initial social and economic handicaps with a good will. It is a pity we are not introduced to that other, complementary freak, Marilyn the plumber, as well; she might have shed some light on her near namesake.[3]

She might indeed, but imagining people at work is not one of Drabble's strengths: Frances has a university appointment, but seems to have no students or faculty colleagues; Clara in *Jerusalem the Golden* does no teaching practice and never attends lectures; and Kate never seems to go to the office. Drabble is cocooned in the intellectual, morally scrupulous, responsible middle class. The spurious social concern for her working-class characters is put to a feminist use of a sort. Denise's husband refuses to let her go back to work as a nurse, though she is 'reluctant to waste all those hard years of training, all those laborious O levels'. The television programme leads the interviewees into 'making fools of themselves', though

> even if you'd had a female director, a female crew, a female television company with female managing directors and a female board, you'd still never get Denise Scooter to say a word in public against her husband, and not because she's frightened of him, but because she thinks it would be treachery. (And she'd be right there, too.)
> Women's lives, progress. What kind of programme ought one to make, anyway?

What indeed? The programme is called 'Women at the Crossroads', but called 'WC' by the men in control. The underlying theme of *The Middle Ground* is the problem of semiotics, or perhaps epistemology. It looks at the devices we use for framing and cataloguing experience: television, literature (including magazines, junk fiction, soap operas, graffiti), codes of dress, history, politics, science (Darwin and Bergson are invoked). Paintings, especially portraits, recur throughout the section written by Hugo: Van Dyck's Duke of Richmond at Kenwood, pictures by Vermeer, de Hooch, Claude Lorraine, Vanmour, Holbein. Hugo's background is, of course, different from Kate's:

> While Kate was reading advertisements in *Woman's Own* and Evelyn Arthur Ransome, Hugo was making his way through *Greenmantle* and *Beau Geste*, through Doughty's *Arabia Deserta*, through Richard Burton, *The Arabian Nights*, *The Seven Pillars of Wisdom*, through Fraser's *Journeys in Kurdistan*. He read also a great deal of poetry; his favourite poet was A. E. Housman, whose landscapes of distant blue remembered hills somehow merged inextricably in his imagination with the mauve horizons and pale-pink brittle icy dawns of the Anatolian plains.

Hugo feels 'modern life is in some mysterious way too fragmented to be comprehensible' and that there is just 'too much data . . . we all know too much, and haven't got the brains to process the info?'

Hugo's story is 'an interlude'. Here is one of Drabble's plays on words: an interlude can mean a story within a story, a pause, an entertainment; all meanings are present at once. A violent and aggressive client of Evelyn's is called 'Irene', the Greek word for peace.

Kate's Iraqi student lodger, Mujid, tells anti-Jewish jokes, which Kate tries to correct by talking about the Second World War, 'of which he in turn seemed surprisingly ignorant. Different languages, different cultures, different history books.' Drabble did have an Arab lodger for a while, and put him to good use in the book.

Mujid can hardly believe Kate's ignorance about the Lebanon, 'the Kurdish question' (and this was written nearly a decade before Saddam Hussein's atrocities against the Kurdish population), about the Ba'ath government, the Palestine Liberation Organization. Kate is puzzled by the mixture of Muslim and Marxist beliefs. Mujid is critical of British television, of what he considers poor coverage of Middle Eastern affairs and pro-Israel, anti-Soviet bias in the newspapers, of the small size and poor quality of English fruit and vegetables. He challenges her assumptions by asking whether the following phenomena are normal, as he finds them in her home: divorce, standing up to eat, women who work so hard? He tries to teach Kate Arabic and the children French, but they are 'too busy doing their French homework'. There is a painful confrontation between Mujid and Jewish friends of Kate's, when the conversation turns to Israel's General Moshe Dayan, Kate Millett (author of the famous feminist book of literary criticism, *Sexual Politics*, 1969), Menachim Begin, then President of Israel, Colonel Gadaffi, the Libyan dictator, the novelist Doris Lessing.

As Gail Efrig notes:

> A great deal of the novel is given over to scenes in which Kate attempts to read herself, and to find out what she should do in the future by evaluation of the past.[4]

Hugo, Kate's journalist friend, wonders:

> Will anyone ever again be able to write with confidence, a book that assumes the significance of one culture only, will anyone ever again be able to stand upright in one nationality? Relativity, comparisons. Well, I have spent a good deal of my life worrying about these things. Culture dies at the interface, one might reasonably fear.

This recapitulates the fear for traditional culture voiced in *The Ice Age*, in which the actuality of the world is pollution and rubbish. The *leitmotif* of *The Middle Ground* is excrement, the production of which is one incontrovertible fact of life on 'this dungy earth'. Drabble here follows Dickens's *Our Mutual Friend* (1864–65), in which human manure is equated with wealth (anticipating Sigmund Freud). In *A Writer's Britain*, Drabble writes that 'Dickens's response to the squalor of the industrial landscape and grimy intricacies of Victorian London is full of ambiguity'[5]; he is the 'great poet of pollution'. Drabble has a similar ambivalent fascination for the détritus of civilization. Interviewed by Clare Boylan in *Cosmopolitan* in 1989, she said:

> I find now that I am fascinated and outraged by rubbish—the peculiar bits of plastic that will form the remnants of our civilisation, the medieval proportions of heaps of rubbish in the street. I'm intrigued by the concepts of 'normal' life and 'normal' marriage. One of my deep beliefs is that we are all very peculiar.

Kate tolerates, even loves, the smell from the sewage bank where she was reared, but this redemptive view is not necessarily that of the author. Kate rejects a novel which says that a mother's life is little more than 'shit and string beans'. This famous phrase comes from the feminist novel by the American academic Marilyn French, *The Women's Room* (1978). Kate thinks soft, milky yellow baby shit 'rather nice really'. Kate is healthier than her friend Sally Jackson, who has gone crazy, 'eating her own shit in middle age'. Despite bad sociology, *The Middle Ground* is a highly intelligent novel, taking on global problems in an illuminating way. Mary Jane Elkins points out that Hugo's is only one voice in this novel, and not Drabble's voice:

> . . . it is only through the combination of voices and perspectives that we as readers are able to hear Drabble's voice and to avoid the error of identifying any one character as her spokesman or even assuming an identification between narrator and author. In other words, to find where the search for order, meaning and pattern leads: we must look to the novel as a whole, to its structure and development . . . in the late novels, plot has been increasingly giving ground to discourse. . . .[6]

Elkins valuably points out that

> there is throughout *The Middle Ground* a feeling of stasis:
> the passage of time in the present tense of the novel becomes
> secondary to inner life and thought. Drabble works to give
> the impression of time standing still. Although in the middle
> of the novel we find several of the major characters doing
> things or going places, Drabble has these events taking place
> simultaneously,[7] and the result is the sense that hardly any
> time is passing.[7]

Again, the problem is survival in a terrible world and the
struggle for health. Sally Jackson is not the only person in
the novel to have a breakdown: Kate's own brother, Peter,
jealous of her fame, sends her poison pen letters and grows
grossly overweight; we hear of a man in Broadmoor who cut
off his wife's head and baked it in the oven; the psychiatrist
who visited him told the story endlessly at dinner parties,
driving his own wife to get up and walk home where
she baked the cat. A mistress of Ted's commits suicide
by drinking spirits of salt and leaving a vitriolic note. Mrs.
Sondersheim appears at a dinner party, unnaturally tense
and silent. Suddenly she describes seeing what seemed to be
a dead baby on the beach at Sierra Leone.

> 'On the waterline.' She paused, but not for effect. 'It was
> almost a skeleton. Rags of skin and flesh. Like a little drifting
> cape, going up and down in the water.' Another pause. 'But
> it wasn't a baby,' she went on in the same dry monotone. 'It
> was only a cat.' She stopped. 'It had a little grinning head,
> with teeth.'

Susan Sondersheim proceeds to lock herself in the bathroom.
Gail Efrig notes that 'her story is really about the children
with syphilis in Sierra Leone.'[8]

Hugo's wife Judith is crazed by the wish for revenge and
is trying to sue for damages after the operation that left her
son David a vegetable. Evelyn has withdrawn sexually from
her husband and winks at his affair with Kate. Neurotic
withdrawal is a temptation for Drabble heroines (Jane, in *The
Waterfall*, lacks the courage to go down the street and ask the
grocer for a pound of sprouts, and Rose in *The Needle's Eye*, tries
to withdraw into poverty and peace). All Drabble heroines,

including Kate, as we shall see, find the courage to face life and to enjoy their food. Susan Sondersheim merely picks at her meal. Then there is Linda Rubenstein, a British woman living in America. Linda is an embattled feminist, who criticizes British women for being so 'passive'. Hugo is listening to the conversation, a 'mini-Babel', over dinner at an overpriced restaurant.

> Tom Rubenstein's sense of perspective appeared to end before Mujid's began, and Linda Rubenstein seemed to consider her own tangential debate the only important debate of history. The ideologies of the late twentieth century mingled but did not mix.

Hugo decides there is 'not a hope' of mutual understanding. Yet Linda's bitter feminist diatribe is treated in a comic mode, the funnier for being deadly accurate. This section is extremely sharp and amusing, if alarming. Kate 'feared that Linda Rubenstein, like Susan Sondersheim so many memorable years ago, was on the verge of some spectacular collapse'. All these women are perfectionists, obsessively tidy. Kate has learned to let go in the company of her husband's parents, who introduce her to art, even if they do allow the cat to 'sleep on the breadboard next to the communal hairbrush, and the mice it failed to catch scamper along the dresser shelves during supper'. They liberate her from the grim rigidity of her own home, and she is warmed by their 'high emotional temperature'. Kate is slapdash and her house a mess, but she recovers her sanity after the grief induced by her abortion. Eventually she cleans up, signifying recovery. After Kate's lover Ted deserts her for 'a woman in Cambridge', Kate finds she is pregnant. She confides in her eldest boy, Mark, who says she must 'get rid of the baby and forget it'. She wonders whether or not to give birth to the baby, but on discovering that it would be born with spina bifida, its back 'split like a kipper', with no bladder or bowel control, she decides to have the abortion. The decision causes her anguish, however, and the section on Kate's feelings about the loss of this foetus is among the most moving things Drabble has ever written. 'Doing the right thing has destroyed me', thinks Kate. During this late pregnancy, when Kate is nearly 40, she is haunted by dreams and night-mares of babies, 'like skinned rabbits'. After the operation, she has 'a year of men', in which she has one disastrous affair after another. These brief chronicles of awful lovers are sad and hilarious: in thumbnail sketches we learn of Patrick, a womanizer, who embarrasses her in bed with baby-talk; Kevin who brings round his washing; Matthew, who lives in squalor but criticizes her lack of hygiene; Adrian, who lets her take him about to expensive hotels and meals, but sulks when he discovers she has booked in her own name, in order to pay by cheque; Emilio, an affected aesthete who turns out to be a phoney, despite his lectureship in art history, with a flat full of grisly junk; an upper-class conman, an alcoholic, and a boastful cook who never lifts a finger in her kitchen. Such demolitions give the female reader a certain *schadenfreude*, it must be admitted.

Kate's children are loveable and healthy, but everybody else in the book seems to have problem children: rebels, misfits. Others are killed in wars. Ted and Evelyn's son Sebastian is a punk, who goes in for

> drinking, drugs, late nights, absent nights, theft. . . . All the Stennets' friends have their own theories about what went wrong, but most agree that it must have something to do with Ted's overbearing personality and ridiculously high expectations.

The novel is full of mad women, dead and abandoned babies, family breakdown. Evelyn visits families where children are neglected and abused, and visits a Day Care Centre where they are cruelly treated. The narrator, through (presumably) Evelyn's consciousness, tells us drily about force-feeding and harsh punishments such as being locked in a cupboard. These are fatherless children whose mothers have to work, and who envy Joan, the woman in charge, because she has 'a proper home and a proper husband to return to'. The emblem of hope among these tragic children is little Rubia from downstairs, the 8-year-old Pakistani girl who makes a 999 call to bring an ambulance: 'Rubia, child of Britain, child of Stoke Newington. How wonderful people are, thought Evelyn, how wonderful.' Evelyn's recovery, like Kate's, is hopeful. Kate and Evelyn (from Evelyn's hospital bed) share an aerial vision of London, with St. Paul's Cathedral in the distance, a city 'always decaying, always renewed . . . the city, the kingdom'. When Kate vigorously cleans her house (compared to the Augean stables) before her ritual celebration, her party, they recall another summer party when there had been 'torrential hot rain'—it was a Day of Judgement party. The religious language, in an apparently secular book, is a reminder of Drabble's real concerns. Kate is putting her house in order, at last, ready to face the future.

The various plots seem at first tenuously connected, but are thematically linked by imagery of health threatened always by disease, excrement, insects, rubbish and dirt.

Kate and Ted both come from underprivileged backgrounds, and

> were both in their way seeking the egalitarian millennium, which would bring security, opportunity and prosperity to all, while rewarding its faithful and elect (such as themselves) with its own special prestige-bearing blessings: a glittering but carefree lifestyle, amusing classless clothes, a freedom of speech and expression hitherto denied to so-called serious people (in other words the licence to use bad language at committee meetings and editorial conferences), a certain gaiety that earlier pioneers of welfare and democracy in the Beveridge era had carefully eschewed, and for which Evelyn, whose inner conviction was that virtue should involve self-denial, had little feeling. The dream of the sixties.

It is not difficult to satirize the '60s from the vantage point of the '80s, but again we hear Drabble rejecting the easy progressivism of her generation. The touchstone is Evelyn, who is viciously attacked and temporarily blinded by one of her clients. The man who throws ammonia in her face sets himself on fire. Roxman observes shrewdly:

> There is an element of the vicariously suffering Christ about [Evelyn], and an element of hell in the brutal man's burning, and his having in some sense caused his own burning.[9]

Evelyn thinks 'people behaved better when they believed.' What are we to think of Philippa Denham, divorced from the faithless Gabriel, now recovered from her breakdown, a 'devout Catholic' convert, who visits the 'terminally ill'?

Ted 'was not a nice man, but he earned a lot'. Ted works for the World Health Organization, and stoically waits for the pandemic he thinks will finish the human race. Ted has had an erratic but successful career, having qualified as a micro-biologist and as a doctor, and he works on 'mosquitoes, monkeys and tropical diseases'. Ted 'likes disasters': the new pandemic will be 'brought about by increasing air travel, increasingly resistant strains of mosquito and rat, brand-new illnesses from new tissue cultures'. (When Drabble wrote *The Middle Ground* AIDS was not yet widespread nor known about.)

> You don't really think medical science is fighting a losing battle, surely, people say to him, and Ted smiles and says no, not really: nevertheless the notion of international disaster excites him, clearly he thinks we deserve it, and that the wrath of God is due to fall once more. Not that he believes in God, of course.

Ted is useful to Kate: he taught her about 'statistics and government reports'. Until then Kate has had 'an almost personal aversion' to them.

> Ted suggested to her that this resistance was caused not by being 'bad at maths' but by the fact that her own situation was so anomalous, sociologically, that she felt that the law of averages threatened her right to exist. She took his point to heart, overcame her suspicions and found a new world of enquiry opened; the particular blossomed into the general, and instead of finding her attention caught by the individual hard case—the rare disease, the crime passionel, the improbable accident, the unexpected success—she found herself entranced by trends, graphs, percentages, emerging patterns, social shifts. The dullest item in the dullest newspaper gleamed with a new interest. She became a dab hand at questioning official statistics and at quarrelling, usually intelligently, with the findings of surveys.

One anecdote about the relationship was originally intended for *The Waterfall*.

> She'd gone to bed early to watch television, taking with her a disgusting little snack consisting of mashed banana, a liberal

quantity of cream, and a sprinkling of small aniseed balls nicked from a child, and had just started eating it when she heard, unexpectedly, Ted's key in the door—he'd decided to drop in to say goodnight on his way home from a meeting. Kate, understandably embarrassed, shoved the plate under the bed, and tried to make Ted welcome, but found herself unable to return his embraces with her usual ardour, smelling strongly as she did of aniseed. Ted, offended, released her, and stepped back into the dish.

Drabble told me she intended to put this incident into the scene where James visits Jane after childbirth, but 'there's nothing romantic about a squashed banana, is there?' she said. I replied that bananas were at least phallic, but she sighed: 'It had to go.' However, as her mother told me, 'She wastes nothing.' She used it four novels later.

The Stennet marriage confirms Kate in her own dislike of marriage, yet she lives with a fantasy that she, the mistress, keeps Evelyn and Ted together. Later, Kate finds a painting called *Psyche locked out of the Palace of Cupid*, and recognizes that

> the castle of love was a prison, a fortress, a tomb, how could she not appreciate her luck in being locked out, in being safe here in the open air? Let her rise and go. (Yet in there, locked within, has she not had the illusion of possessing infinite space?).

This is a characteristically qualified statement. Kate, however, ends the novel without a lover, but with friends. Earlier, she has a mid-life crisis and doubts her rôle as a spearhead of the women's movement.

> The commercial exploitation of Women began to horrify her in a new way. One could sell anything these days, she began to think, so long as it was angry enough.

Kate is hardly worried at all about the 'old-fashioned code of sexual guilt', but worries terribly about 'the newly-forged code of feminist guilt', wondering whether one was merely the updated version of the other. Like earlier Drabble heroines, Kate feels the lack of 'guidelines for behaviour'. Reflecting on her father's life, Kate remembers that 'Women do not have to wheel barrowloads of contraceptives, or crawl on their hands and knees through underground sewers, or wade thigh-high in torrents of effluent.' Kate is her father's daughter, but the rôle of the parents within the novel is nevertheless strange, almost to the point of evasion. It is explained that Kate does not have much time to see her ageing parents these days. Indeed, they never appear in the novel at all, except in connection with Kate's unpleasant childhood. When she goes back to her home district of London (Romley, reminiscent of Romney Marshes, probably intended as somewhere in unfashionable Essex), we meet the current headmistress of Kate's old school (which does not seem to have been amalgamated into a mixed comprehensive, as most old secondary modern schools were by 1980, when the novel appeared), but we get no news of her parents or records of any conversations with them. We never learn whether they are proud of her, or jealous of her, like Peter.

Commentators have noticed how dogs feature in *The Ice Age*. There are dogs in *The Middle Ground*, too. In one of Kate's worst moments, a dog pisses on her skirt. Yet Kate's generosity is shown when she takes care of a dog for a while, until its owner comes to collect it.

There is satire on pretentious or failed art, as usual:

> Sam Goldman was a South African, whose early black comedies were set in his native land: thence he moved to racism in Britain, though his last piece, a qualified success, had been about technological breakdown and cannibalism in a high-rise block in the year 2000.

Now Sam is moving 'out into the apocalyptic, the unknown'. The names of the characters are the tired old Greek icons: 'Tiresias, Cassandra, Philoctetes'. The set is 'pseudo-classical', with a motor-bike, an old-fashioned Victorian camera on a tripod, and some scattered pieces of futuristic furniture. The play is dull. Bits of machinery fall off, 'presumably prophesying the death of technology of which Sam seemed so fond these days'. After this awful evening, Tom Rubenstein 'conceded that British acting was still the best in the world, one of the last remaining fields in which Britain still reigned supreme'.

How do we take this? Do we share Drabble's mockery

of such solemn rubbish, or are we intended to weep at the degeneracy of theatrical art, as we were in the case of Mike Morgan in *The Ice Age*? At the show is one of the new iconoclastic journalists who digs out such facts as that 'a [government] minister has an embarrassing speech defect, or that another has a delinquent daughter'. Kate's husband has his moment of validation when he calls this journalist 'a rat'.

This scurrility is paralleled by the graffiti Kate finds in London, expressing obscenity, racism and violent hatreds. Kate reads them as symptoms of a social disease:

> Sensibilities were inflamed, catching insults, where none were intended: an ideological epidemic had swept through Britain, perhaps through the world. The raw membrane caught every passing disease. Swollen organs of indignation impeded natural functioning on every side. And what was the answer to that? This is the disease of capitalism, Mujid would no doubt say.... And would be right? God knows, for I certainly don't. Oh lord, thought Kate, first I had a Freudian nervous breakdown through Ted and that baby business, and now I'm having a Marxist nervous breakdown through Mujid. To hell with them both, she said to herself crossly. . . .

This is characteristic Drabble writing: the physical, social and spiritual are elided in one of her extended metaphors (first used in *The Needle's Eye*, rather clumsily, but since refined). The 'swollen organs of indignation' is a portmanteau phrase, suggesting anger as a disease of the body politic and by implication the newspapers ('organs' of opinion). As usual, confronted with an existential dilemma, the protagonist sighs, 'God knows', which is an unacknowledged form of prayer. Kate's hopeless shrug reminds us of Rose in *The Needle's Eye*, rejecting religious neurosis, saying to herself, 'to hell with Bunyan', and finding a 'neurotic heroic nonchalance'. Drabble's concern with the ecology and pollution, brilliantly imaged throughout the book, is a metaphor for the spiritual state of mankind. Here social, physical and spiritual health are brought explicitly together in what Lynn Veach Sadler calls 'Drabble's strange combination of the transcendent and the real'.[10] This 'strange combination' constitutes Drabble's importance as a writer. She ponders the 'eternal verities' and wonders whether they can still be true.

Evelyn, Kate's *alter ego,* asks, 'Why expect results, progress, success, a better society? All we can do is to join the ranks of the caring rather than the uncaring.' Evelyn is a reader of Meister Eckhart, whose message is 'Strip away all creatures so that nothing can comfort you except God.' The tension here is the same as Rose Vassiliou's, between the spiritual and the secular worlds. Gail Efrig observes, wisely, that Kate's emptiness is the emptiness of the good human secularist in modern Britain.[11] She believes this book continues the examination of British society that began with *The Needle's Eye* and continued with *The Ice Age.* True, but beneath the social phenomena lies the permanent spiritual plight of man, torn between soul and body.

Drabble herself is an active Vice-Patron of the Child Psychology Trust, an organization set up to observe and treat disturbance in children. She has 'joined the ranks of the caring'.

We find the expected obeisance to Wordsworth; Ted misquotes 'On the naming of places', 'There is an eminence': he says 'You have so loved me, that no place on earth/ Can ever be a solitude to me.' A page later, we read the words of the omniscient narrator:

> Neither of them ever found out how significantly they had misquoted Wordsworth. The grand old man had been a step ahead of them. Even clever Isobel had not spotted it, a lapse that would have annoyed her had she ever discovered it, for she liked nothing more than correcting other people's quotations. An interesting lapse.

Wordsworth actually wrote:

> She who dwells with me, whom I have loved
> With such communion that no place on earth
> Can ever be a solitude to me.

The 'significance' of the mistake is that Ted and Isobel interpret the lines egotistically, greedy for love; but the poem celebrates love given, rather than love received.

As in earlier novels, Drabble finally puts her faith in life itself. I am grateful for Efrig's exegesis of the bay tree Kate buys at the end of the novel. Efrig writes:

139

There can be little doubt that it stands for England. On a gold medal cast for Queen Elizabeth 1 in 1588, to celebrate the defeat of the Armada, the queen's goldsmith modelled the island planted with a large bay tree at its centre. *Non ipsa pericula tangunt*: no dangers touch here, says the motto; the bay is eternal . . . green, glossy, flourishing, the bay tree lives and breathes. More than a promise or a hope, it is life itself.[12]

There are other overtones. As the Prayer Book has it, 'I myself have seen the ungodly in great power and flourishing like a green bay tree': we have to accept evil in the world, as a part of sublunary life. Yet the 'bays' or laurel leaves are also the crown of the poet, the literary thinker. The final words of *The Middle Ground* are 'She rises', in resurrection and renewal. The ending of *The Middle Ground*, a party which is a downmarket version of the one in *Mrs. Dalloway*, is far from trivial: it is a paean to human courage and resilience, to faith in the God-given gift of life, and implicitly to 'the holiness of the heart's affections and the truth of the imagination', Margaret Drabble's abiding concerns.

NOTES

1. Lynn Veach Sadler, *Margaret Drabble*, p. 118.
2. Susanna Roxman, *Guilt and Glory*, p. 120.
3. Roxman, p. 117.
4. Gail Efrig, 'The Middle Ground', in Dorey Schmidt (ed.), *Margaret Drabble: Golden Realms*, p. 182.
5. Margaret Drabble, *A Writer's Britain*, p. 207.
6. Mary Jane Elkins, 'Alenoushka's Return: Motifs and Movement in Margaret Drabble's *The Middle Ground*' in Cronan Rose (ed.), *Critical Essays*, p. 170.
7. Ibid.
8. Efrig, p. 176.
9. Roxman, p. 118.
10. Sadler, p. 123.
11. Efrig, p. 181.
12. Efrig, p. 184.

10

The Radiant Way (1987)

During the seven year gap, Drabble was re-editing the *Oxford Companion to English Literature* (which she nicknamed 'Ockle'). *The Radiant Way* is a wise and wonderful book, but it puzzled some of her faithful readers because it seemed to take a new direction. It is dense, thickly plotted; there is an enormous cast of characters. Readers could no longer easily find or identify with Drabble woman, or find the nuclear family.

Yet despite apparent discontinuity, the trademarks are still there: Drabble woman becomes a threesome who met at Cambridge. Drabble writes:

> In the 1950s, one of the surest ways forward for an intellectual young woman . . . a socially disadvantaged young woman from the provinces was through Oxford, through Cambridge. Not through Manchester or Leeds, or Durham, or Bristol, but through Oxford or Cambridge.

Drabble is indeed the poet not only of maternity but of Cambridge, offering cosy nostalgia to those of us who share her privileged education, doubtless producing baffled rage in those who went to Manchester, Leeds, Durham or Bristol. This is also a novel about 'the two nations', in Benjamin Disraeli's phrase: smart life among the television journalists in London, working-class life in the north. The working-class characters are treated comically, like charwomen in old copies of *Punch*. Shirley Harper, who as a girl chose sex instead of scholarship, is stuck in the provinces. She *is* sick of

> secondhand opinions, . . . echoes from overheard conversations, . . . phrases from advertisements and tabloid newspapers, and yet to Shirley there was perhaps something comfortable, despite all, something reassuring about the hands of

141

cards, . . . the predictable, ancient jokes . . . there was safety here, of a sort, safety in repetition, safety in familiar faces and frustrations, and warmth . . . and community of a sort . . . the society she had discovered as a teenager, when she would slip surreptitiously out of the icy silence of Abercorn Avenue, where the clock ticked relentlessly on the kitchen wall, where Liz propped her textbooks against the Peak Freen biscuit tin on the kitchen table. . . .

Characters from the previous novels pop up in London, where everybody knows everybody else by ties of elective affinity, even if their roots are in other places less privileged. Kinship and archaeology inform this novel: Shirley's daughter Celia is studying the Brigantes. There are embedded quotations from Shakespeare and Milton and Jonathan Swift, and guests at a party may be about to 'turn into swine' under the influence of drink, like Circe's. The Porter's speech in Shakespeare's *Macbeth* is ironically invoked, suggesting that evil may be abroad:

There they gathered, the faithless priest, the investor about to hang himself in the expectation of plenty, the physician who will not be able to heal herself, the director who lacks all direction.

(echoing Yeats's cry in 'The Second Coming', 'The best lack all conviction and the worst/ Are full of a passionate intensity'), with a pun on 'direction':

. . . the historian who denies the existence of history, the Jewish scholar of early Renaissance Christian iconography, the deaf man who hears voices, the woman about to be taken in adultery.

The Minotaur, the labyrinth of the self, and Ariadne supply a running thread of images. A middle-class drop-out called Jilly Fox becomes the victim of a serial murderer who chops off women's heads, and she is compared with Medusa (and she turns Alix's kind heart to stone). The references to mythology and history are not excrescences, but an important part of the whole. Liz the psychiatric expert gives a talk on 'the family romance'. Although *The Radiant Way* is partly a 'condition-of-England' novel, its implicit metaphor is Yggdrasil, the tree of life: in it Drabble explores the historical roots of the irrational, the pathological, as well as contributing a disillusioned analysis of political faith in Britain in the '80s.

The main characters are Liz, a psychiatrist, Alix who scrapes a living as a part-time teacher of English at a prison, and Esther, an art historian. (The scholarship here is precise and rich; it helps if you understand Italian and have some knowledge of lesser Italian Renaissance painters, all of whom can be checked in named reference books. For those who have the background, these sections are particularly satisfying.) Esther thinks of

> the greengrocery—pears, apples, peaches, marrows—with which Crivelli liked to adorn his subjects, and thought that this time she would dwell more on the phallic and the uterine as represented by the gaily coloured little arrows that so happily and decoratively perforated the sultry, smiling, androgynous Saint Sebastian on the Virgin's left, and by the Virgin's appearance to Gabriel from a vaginal slit in the sky, wittily echoed by the Saint's own red rocky womblike bolt hole. They would like that in Birmingham.[1]

Esther wonders whether a polyptich is the *Madonna Della Pesca* (peach) or the *Madonna Delle Pesce* (fish). An eldritch note is struck, however, by a character called Claudio Volpe, who seems to have strayed in from a novel of magic realism: he claims, at a serious conference, to have seen a werewolf. His audience wonder whether he is talking about deconstruction. (The intellectual jokes in this novel are rewarding to the literate; and once again, Drabble is asking, with Ibsen and Freud, what is the relation between nature and nurture, between instinct and culture?) It is suggested Claudio is mad. He has been the love of Esther's life, but we learn later that all her relationships have consisted of an effort to avoid normal sexual intercourse. Esther believes 'we are all very, very sick.' She talks obsessively about her potted palm, as if it were a pet, presumably to hide her real emotions or lack of them. Esther is an outsider because she is Jewish. Liz is an outsider because of working-class origins. Alix is an outsider because her parents are liberals, who Alix is convinced are cranks, out of the same stable as Rosamund Stacey's, and she has been to a boarding school which sounds faintly like Drabble's own, except in that it is co-educational.

> . . . her parents . . . were . . . harmless, mild, Labour-voting, CND-supporting, Fabian pamphlet-reading intellectuals, of a species that Alix now knew to be far from extinct . . . the school . . . had been nonconformist, faintly progressive, certainly egalitarian in its religious and social complexion: it had offered a liberal, secularised, healthy co-education, and had on its foundation in the 1860s set out to attract the children of vegetarians, Quakers, freethinkers, pacifists, Unitarians, reformers. . . .

But the pupils have become prosperous, and 'what had . . . seemed strange, in her girlhood, had been her parents' quaint socialist ideals, which had caused her such embarrassment.' Alix's own college at first strikes her as 'somewhat dimly conformist, with long brown corridors' (the corridors of Newnham, indeed memorable, recur in fictions by the Drabble sisters). Alix reads English, marries young. We are not surprised that she falls madly in love with her baby son, and rejects her unsatisfactory husband. He conveniently drowns and Alix marries a socialist schoolteacher who has published a working-class novel but failed to progress. Brian would rather be teaching great literature than collecting the reminiscences of the unemployed and publishing them in co-operative magazines, but eventually even such projects are taken away as he is made redundant. Poor Brian represents an obsolescent expertise, an outdated faith. Alix, disillusioned, is embarrassed to see him standing in the street with a yellow plastic bucket collecting money for the striking miners in 1984. The self-deception of Brian's friends approaches 'mass psychosis', and Brian has started using the word 'élitist'. Alix has revolved in her own head a debate as to the validity of 'progressive' socialism and found it wanting. Her own part-time job is under threat.

Drabble's continued analysis, bordering on satire, of the socialist, pacificist values of her youth is a painful growth; yet she has not turned to the right. She is a member not only of the human rights protest movement, Charter 88, but of the 'June 20th Group', where writers such as John Mortimer, Angela Carter, Antonia Fraser and Ian McEwan met as a counterblast to Thatcherism. Eventually Alix falls in love with Brian's friend, Otto, an academic and he with her, but they do nothing about it. Otto goes to Washington to teach and Alix suffers in silence, apart from telling a colleague, who is equally unhappy in love: Polly confides her own passion for 'an unlikely much-married somewhat disreputable antique dealer' who she doesn't really like or respect, 'but I can't help going to bed with him.' Alix and Polly discuss the complications in the sex lives of emancipated women today.

Alix is to become a leading character in the sequel, *A Natural Curiosity*. Then there is Stephen Cox, a traveller and writer, in the same mould as David the geologist in *The Realms of Gold* and Hugo the traveller and journalist in *The Middle Ground*, men who live for their intellectual passions and seem to do without women. We are promised a third novel in the sequence, about Stephen Cox in Kampuchea.

The three women meet more or less regularly. Their common experience at an (unnamed) Cambridge college, their differing perspectives, enable them to converse on a high level. And in this book we do at last see people at work, successfully realized.

The chief character here is Liz Headleand (Head-land? a thrusting promontory? Or should it be 'Heed-land'?) Liz has been divorced, and in true Drabble fashion does not get an orgasm till she tries Charles, her second husband. At the party Liz gives at the start of the novel, in the New Year of 1980, both her husbands are present, and Liz has the secret pleasure of knowing that two other men she has slept with are in the room. The fifth is a Dutchman with whom she shared a wild Channel crossing, whose name she never knew, but who turns up on the same aircraft as Esther later on, though Esther of course does not know about him and Liz. This coincidence may be an arbitrary plot device, or it may be what Drabble believes to be coincidence's 'long arm'. As Liz says, 'we are all deeply superstitious'. In her agnostic way, she too waits for 'revelation'.

Liz's rôle as psychiatrist is that of secular priestess; we read of Joseph O'Toole, priest turned psychotherapist (in real life figures such as Carl Rogers and Abraham Maslow trained as priests). We see her with her patients, yet she cannot cope with her own distress when her husband announces he wants a divorce after twenty years and two daughters. Liz, who considers herself 'biologically a peasant', is jealous of Charles's new woman, Lady Henrietta Latchett (for whose family, it is revealed, Liz's mother once worked as a domestic servant). Henrietta is a mere sketch of a character, bland, an exploiter. There is now a recognizable Drabble Britain, made up of: actors, television journalists, writers, who live in London; their unsuccessful relatives in the North; depressed, agoraphobic mothers; Quakers, socialists and other Nonconformists who agonize over moral and social problems; hungry Oxbridge-educated women; women who take a long time and several partners before they achieve orgasm, but always worship their babies; stern, detached, enigmatic males, and their opposites, the sexy, irresistible lovers, usually unsuitable or unreliable. Lady Henrietta is the first aristocratic character (apart from, possibly, Frances Wingate's mother in *The Realms of Gold*) in Drabble's world, and belongs with Dickens's Doodles and Coodles, privileged but useless; there is no effort to understand her, except the information that a dragon of a nanny nearly frightened her out of her wits. Her marriage to Charles does not last, though by the time it has collapsed Liz, like Kate Armstrong in *The Middle Ground*, has decided that life without sex and its complications suits her very well.

Charles is the nastiest type of power-hungry tycoon, who enjoys sacking people and gets his come-uppance when he is himself made redundant, but with an enormous golden handshake.

Liz and Shirley have lived in isolation with an eccentric mother who acts as though she were mad, so anxious is she to have no contact with neighbours. We recognize a more extreme case like that of Clara Maugham's mother in *Jerusalem the Golden* and Kate Fletcher's in *The Middle Ground*. But Rita reads Dickens and Trollope, she encourages her daughters to be ambitious. Liz chooses deferred gratification, Shirley follows her instincts.

In mid-career, Liz wonders about her efficacy as therapist.

I am as serviceable as I ever was. But how can I be, when I know that I do not understand my own problems, when I know that I do not know, when I have been obliged to admit that I do not stand on solid ground, when my own patterns are obscure to me?

The wounded healer. But that is another concept: that is the concept of the healer whose knowledge of the malady springs from a fellow sickness, from a diagnosed fellow-sickness.

Is there, perhaps an analogy with the faithless priest? Liz, a child of the North of England and daughter of an irreligious house, does not know much about Catholicism, but has read her Graham Greene and dimly recalls the notion that even the unworthy vessel, the doubting vessel, can minister the true sacrament. Her rational self accepts this as rational: it is the nature of the healing, not the spirit of the healer, that is of value both to rational and to religious man. . . .

She decides she has 'a spiritual body odour'. She has deceived her own training analyst, by denying any memories before 4 years old. But we learn that Liz has suppressed the memory (revealed when she returns to Northam to sort out her dead mother's effects) of her own sexual excitement when tickled by her father. Never spoken of, he had committed suicide after being convicted of indecent exposure. Her mother's rigidity becomes explicable at last. Liz, in adolescence, has 'dreamed of tortures, imprisonments, knives, daggers, dark towers. Wounds, blows, penetrations. Even now, she does not like to look back on them. They continue to shame, these fantasies.' Liz's sexual relationship with Charles is one of submission to his desire for dominance, even punishment. She recognizes that Charles 'has replaced the fantastic, punishing father of her childhood', though at this stage Liz has no idea what it was her father had done. Now she has to learn to 'disbelieve the meaning, the very existence, of their mutual past'. In earlier Drabble novels, the interest in 'perversity' was playful, though by the time of *The Needle's Eye* there are hints of masochism in Rose. In *The Radiant Way* and in *A Natural Curiosity* she investigates the perversity, the criminal tendencies that lie within us all; but she never explicitly calls it original sin in this novel.

Liz's patients include a mother who has murdered her child. The mortuary assistant who deals with Jilly's corpse

(which has been dumped in Alix's broken-down car)

> had been educated in a Quaker school in York, and as a boy
> had been disturbed by descriptions of heads displayed above
> the city gates, displayed and left to rot, the hair falling away,
> the teeth bravely grinning at the weather: now they returned
> to grin at him. Heads, haunches, forequarters, set upon poles.
> No, no, no thank you, said Mike Gittings, tossing in his
> history-troubled sleep.

History, the bloody history of the race, horrid images of human sacrifice, trouble all the sleepers in this book. The paintings of Christian martyrs studied by Esther are full of wounds, blood, torture. Claudio, dying, talks of 'Gorgon and the Medusa and Géricault and Demigorgon and Salome and the Bessi of Thrace'.

Drabble does not explain this jumble of ideas, though the associative links are clear. The Gorgon was the Medusa, with snakes for hair, whose look turned the viewer to stone; the French painter Géricault (1791–1824) painted a picture now in the Louvre called 'The Raft of the Medusa', which shows survivors of a shipwreck stretched out in their last agonies. There were rumours of cannibalism on board. 'Demigorgon' is a mistake for Demogorgon, the terrible deity whose very name brought disaster if spoken. This deity is believed to be identical with the Infernal Power of the ancients, mentioned in Lucan's *Pharsalia* (see Chapter 11, note 2). Demogorgon, however, is also divided into an evil spirit and a good one: according to Ariosto (1474–1533), Demogorgon was a king of the elves and fays who lived on the Himalayas. He is thus a terrible god and a pleasant superstition: which? Salome is famous for having demanded the head of John the Baptist on a charger, or dish; and the Bessi of Thrace are also unexplained in the text, but in their land was the oldest oracle of Dionysos. Dionysos was the god under whose influence the Bacchae, in the play by the Greek dramatist Euripides (c. 484–407 BC), tore to pieces the son of their chief priestess who, disguised as a woman, spied on their rites. The dichotomy in this novel and its sequel is what Friedrich Nietzsche, in *The Birth of Tragedy* (1900), categorized as the Appollonian, or rational, and the Dionysiac, the savage instinct which demands blood sacrifices. Nietzsche wrote a book called *Beyond Good and Evil*; Jilly declares that 'evil and good are one', and writes in a letter to Alix that

> Crime is not, sin is not; evil is not; all is good, all is holy. The winter solstice is now, and forever, and never, for the light shines for ever, in eternal glory, and we are consumed and not consumed in everlasting fire.

Liz, the practical physician, puts this flight down to drugs; but the language is also that of occult religion and mysticism. Drabble has probably read the famous work by E. R. Dodds, *The Greeks and the Irrational*. It is always unwise not to check Drabble's references, integral to her webs of imagery; it does not do to under-estimate her learning, which can give hidden thematic clues.

Liz has a modern digital clock, but the passing of time, imaged by flowing sand, is invoked by the egg-timer in Mrs. Orme's kitchen, which expresses 'the sands of time'. Mrs. Orme reminds Brian and Alix of the amusements, the petty craftwork, of my own childhood: woolly bobbles made from cardboard milk-bottle tops, French knitting done on a wooden cotton reel, 'unravelled wool, patchwork, scrap rugs. A way of life, a culture'.

In this novel we get characters' views of each other. To Alix's eye, Shirley exhibits a 'habitual confidence, a knowing-ness, a town-smartness'. She admires Shirley's fashionable suit. Shirley's sister Liz thinks Shirley looks ridiculous:

> Why was she wearing that department-store suit and that strange shirt with a watch-strap pattern and a big bow? It was hardly appropriate for an evening with old friends. . . .

Shirley's husband Cliff is related to Alix's husband Brian. Shirley and Liz are both in search of relatives and Liz is in quest of herself. But she finds out that she is a sort of 'reverse Cinderella', whose dénouement is less than glorious. Despite the pressure of her scientific work, Liz as a student had read her mother's nineteenth-century novels and tried 'to learn the book of Job by heart' (perhaps improbably). But, as in *The Middle Ground*, the theme is health and sickness, and the pattern is the Quest Novel and the discovery of long-lost relatives: the family romance.

The Radiant Way, an infant reader, in common with

Drabble's aureate imagery, suggests infinite possibilities, a road to success. When a child learns to read, it is inducted into culture. Charles and Liz have shared cultural and social privilege, but the child of Wordsworth's 'Immortality Ode' is now the Freudian child, with sexual secrets.

In September 1983 Drabble wrote to me about *The Radiant Way*: 'I have a good plan for a new novel, which will be very different and long and precious, and not at all journalistic.'

Reviewers, who are generally impercipient about Drabble on first reading, labelled it 'superficial' and 'shapeless'. As Nora Foster Stovel says of this novel:

> Discovering the redeeming design beneath the depressing detail is harder than ever . . . for . . . [the novel] portrays Drabble's darkest vision ever. Where the vision of *The Middle Ground* was squalid and even excremental—its personal and national midlife crises symbolised appropriately by the central symbol of sewage—. . . contemporary life in *The Radiant Way* is indeed demonic.[2]

Stovel analyses the motif of severed heads and suggests that women may be divided, in the eyes of male beholders, into 'head or rationality and torso or sexuality', like the cockatrice in Jilly's psychotic painting and mentioned in her letter. The novel 'chronicles the potency of evil in both private and public life'.[3] Stovel valuably analyses the significance of Claudio Volpe as 'werewolf' himself, who may have possessed the soul of the murderer, Paul Whitmore, pointing out that the werewolf is another divided creature, 'the human beast, divided between mind and body, angel and devil, as symbolized by the monsters of mythology'.[4]

The horror builds, while Esther and Liz look at small dead fishes in a polluted canal, and think it may be a portent of the end of the world.

Yet, for Stovel, 'Jilly, the modern martyr, is a female scapegoat figure, whose suicide, like that of Stephen Ollerenshaw in *The Realms of Gold*, purifies the spiritual disease which plagues the populace.'[5]

But has Jilly committed suicide, by conniving at her own murder? We are not told.

The novel ends with the three old friends taking one of their habitual walks together, in the country, renewed. But despite the upbeat ending, the overriding impression is of a terrible world, through which the characters must pick their way as best they can. If harmony is achieved, it is at the cost of human sacrifice.

In *The Radiant Way* Drabble mentions *Painting in Naples from Caravaggio to Giordano*, the catalogue of a remarkable exhibition at the Royal Academy, London, in 1982.[6] This catalogue of religious horrors, rather than Crivelli (an earlier painter from a more northern part of Italy) supplies many of the images Drabble suggests in the text: crucifixions; incest (Lot and his daughters); Cavallino's two different versions of Judith with the (severed) head of Holofernes; Apollo and Marsyas (a scene of flaying alive, interpreted by early Christians as vain pride suitably punished, later as a symbol of divine harmony triumphing over earthly passions, light and reason winning over primitive darkness); the dead Christ figures traditionally called Pietàs; gladiatorial fights; John the Baptist's severed head on its charger, depicted by Pieter Paul Rubens (1577–1640) and the Italian artist Preti, who also gives us a Saint Sebastian pierced by arrows; Giordano's St. Michael vanquishing the devil, who howls in agony as he is speared and trodden on; and, most interesting to us of all, Giordano's 'Phineas and his companions turned to stone', all in full colour. Perseus, looking sternly in a different direction, holds his sword in his right hand. In his left is a waxy-yellow female head, its mouth open in a scream. Instead of writhing snakes, the hair is tolerably realistic, as if permed into corkscrew curls.[7] The features are small, rather beautiful. We recognize her. It is the head, as memorably described in Drabble's text, of Jilly Fox.

NOTES

1. This picture is in the National Gallery, London, No. 668. The Blessed (not Saint) Gabriel, who died in 1456, was Superior of the Convent of San Francisco ad Alto, Ancona. The Virgin appeared to him in a wood near the friary. The painting is decorated, characteristically, with fruit and flowers, in accordance with traditional symbolism, in which fruit represents the twelve fruits of the spirit: love, joy, peace,

long-suffering, gentleness, goodness, faith, meekness, patience, modesty, temperance and chastity.

The paintings of the Venetian Crivelli (whose work is more typical of the Sienese school than the Venetian) belong to this earlier tradition in which the iconography is stylized and conventional; he was already old-fashioned in his own day. Crivelli died in 1500, when Michelangelo was 25.

2. Nora Foster Stovel, *Margaret Drabble: Symbolic Moralist*, p. 188.

3. Stovel, p. 190.

4. Stovel, p. 192. Olga Kenyon tells me Drabble told her that Volpe is based on the Italian scholar Mario Praz, author of *The Romantic Agony*, who used to call on 'demonic forces' when lecturing.

5. Stovel, p. 196.

6. The exhibition of Neapolitan art had a powerful impact on those of us who saw it, and its catalogue, *Painting in Naples from Caravaggio to Giordano*, offers images totally different—more realistic, more disturbing. The 'smiling, sultry, androgynous Saint Sebastians' are more common in this later period. The catalogue shows a suffering Saint Sebastian by Mattia Preti (1613–99). These baroque paintings by seventeenth-century Neapolitan artists are alive with violent energies— and the energies invoked tend to be destructive, despite their avowed religious messages. The baroque is more ambiguous than the *quattro-centro* in its iconographies, because it embraces mythological as well as religious themes. There is a strong appeal to the sadistic voyeur. Secular concerns overlap the overtly religious messages. This is all of a piece with *The Radiant Way*, which like the whole of Drabble's *oeuvre* asks what place religion has in life; what are the claims of fleshly nature (which includes sexuality and violence) and what are those of the spirit?

7. In Greek mythology Perseus slew Medusa the Gorgon, whose glance turned the viewer to stone, with the aid of a mirror. He chopped off her head, which instead of hair had writhing snakes.

11

A Natural Curiosity (1989)

The paintings of Crivelli are in the main on traditional religious subjects. The pictures in *Painting in Naples from Caravaggio to Giordano*, which supplies the unforgettable image of St. Agatha clutching a bloody towel to where her breasts have been severed, mentioned in *The Radiant Way*, are even more allegorical and more explicit pictorially than earlier ones. Just as St. Michael trampling the devil signifies the triumph of goodness, so the beheading of the Medusa by Perseus was frequently interpreted as a symbol of Christ triumphing over the Prince of evil. In the Renaissance this struggle was called the conflict between 'passion' or instinct and 'reason' or culture and morality. Nietzsche gave new labels to the old concepts. Drabble's treatment of the theme in these two novels is a logical development of her earlier work; *The Radiant Way* and *A Natural Curiosity* are about the persistence of evil in the world, and traditional religion is, as in *The Ice Age*, invoked. Charles Headleand, in *A Natural Curiosity*, has fallen on hard times. Divorced from his third wife, Henrietta, he lives in a small flat. He reads the Koran (which seems to be driving people mad, he thinks) and is driven to steal a Gideon Bible from a hotel as a corrective. In a scene which is comic yet serious in intent, he discovers Mark's Gospel, Chapter 8, verses 34 to 38:

> Whosoever will come after me, let him deny himself, and take up his cross and follow me.
>
> For whosoever will save his life shall lose it; but whosoever shall lose his life for my sake and the gospel's, the same shall save it.

> For what shall it profit a man if he gain the whole world,
> and lose his own soul?
> Or what shall man give in exchange for his soul?
> Whosoever therefore shall be ashamed of me and of my
> words in this adulterous and sinful generation; of him also
> shall the Son of Man be ashamed, when he cometh in the
> glory of his Father with the holy angels.

Charles recognizes that he is of the 'adulterous and sinful
generation'. Drabble herself writes: 'This is not a political
novel. More a pathological novel. A psychotic novel. Sorry
about that. It won't happen again. Sorry.' Elsewhere, she
writes:

> People want to believe in an ordered regular world of faithful
> married couples, legitimate children, normal sex, legal behav-
> iour, decent continuity, and they will go to almost any lengths
> to preserve this faith. Any suggestion that 'real life' is other-
> wise tends to be greeted as 'melodramatic' or 'implausible'.
> Solicitors know better. The police know better. Social work-
> ers know better. Doctors . . . know better. The subplots fester,
> break out, infect strangers. Dark blotches spread. Life is more
> like an old-fashioned melodramatic novel than we care to
> know.

This passage expresses one of the core themes of this novel.
'Subplots fester' is a characteristic Drabble elision, a mixed
metaphor. In this novel she continues the exploration begun
in *The Radiant Way* of the roots of behaviour, but though Alix
Bowen's search for motive satisfies her, we are left with the
impression that the quest has been futile. At 15, Alix had
noticed that systems provided their own answers, none of
which need bear any relation to any other system, nor could
they be checked. 'So religion had survived, so ideologies
survived, in blatant defiance of *how things were*.' She does
remember a spinster schoolmistress who taught her that all
souls were equal in the sight of God and the only valid
principle was love. At the end of the novel, Alix bathes naked
in a stream.

> She sees a vivid flash of blue. A kingfisher. Her heart leaps
> with delight. She knows she is peculiarly blessed. . . . She
> rises, dripping, newly baptised. . . . She gazes at the trees. . . .
> The sacred grove, the sacred pool. It is an old friendly place

... she strides barefoot back up the track, toward her car. Somebody is waiting for her. An old man leans on the gate, as he has leant for centuries. His face is gnarled and wrinkled. He is dark and small of stature, as his people were and are. ... His smile is broad, knowing, capacious, unsurprised.

Who, what is he? An old countryman? A Celt? A nature spirit? Wordsworth's Leech-gatherer? A figure out of Rudyard Kipling or Thomas Hardy's works? It does not matter. Alix has had a Drabblean mystical experience: the kingfisher is a fleeting vision of the miraculous in nature, and in life; she is renewed; she meets some sort of symbol of permanence of the race. And Alix has refrained from adultery with Otto, who has 'honourably' taken his wife and children to Washington with him. In this novel the three protagonists are separated: Liz remains in London; Esther has gone to live in Bologna with Claudio's sister Elena, a Marxist-lesbian-feminist of whom Esther is eventually to tire; and Brian Bowen has had to move back to Yorkshire for a job. There is a disused bear pit in the region, where people were once entertained by the torture of captive bears. The main plot concerns Alix's visits to Paul Whitmore, the serial murderer and decapitator of women. The central mystery of the novel is that Paul (who lived in the same block of flats as Esther, which is one of the reasons for her flight) is a mild-mannered, lonely vegetarian (perhaps because his father was a butcher). Paul's interest in severed heads arises from a passionate, almost scholarly, interest in Celtic Britain, in early history, in pre-Christian religions. Alix discovers that in the Celtic religion the severed head was as important as the Cross is in Christianity. It emerges that Paul had a twin sister who died, that his mother ('a mad woman, a fury, a harpy, a gorgon') abused and neglected Paul. In a somewhat unconvincing pair of scenes, Alix finds out that Paul's mother, Angela, works as a dog-breeder. Her door-knocker is a female *tete coupée*, 'a common design . . . Alix had never before thought of seeing it as a Medusa, as a Celtic offering'. Alix finds out on a second visit that some of the dogs are abominably treated: the ironically-named Angela starves them to death; a decapitated horse's head hangs just out of their reach. This is no arbitrary motif; Alix says at one point that in Celtic mythology wheels were thought to be 'apotropaic'. She does not gloss the word. From the Oxford English Dictionary we learn that it means 'having power to avert evil influence or bad luck'. The illustrative quotation mentions that 'the sacrifice of the October horse . . . had also a naturalistic and apotropaic character.' The Romans sacrificed a horse to Mars every 15 October. The head was cut off and decked with cakes. (Drabble's subtext of recondite learning is formidable.) Alix reports Angela for this cruelty and she is eventually fined £120. Esther and Liz agree that Paul has 'clearly been unhinged by maternal neglect, by maternal hatred, by punitive discrimination in his early years'. Liz reflects that Paul's father is a decent person, that many children grow up fairly normal without any parental kindness, or at least do not become murderers. Liz has no better explanation: 'She does not claim to understand the pathology of Paul Whitmore. Like Alix, she tends not to believe in evil. So Alix's version is as good as any.' Alix herself admits that she has proved nothing by her discoveries.

> I've just confirmed my own prejudices about human nature. I've been travelling around a closed circuit. A closed system. Me and my murderer together. It wasn't a theorem, it was a circuit.

Liz (who to Nora Foster Stovel is a white witch[1]) is the physician-priestess who has failed to heal herself, though time and nature have helped; Liz takes pleasure in her step-grand-daughter, Cornelia Headleand (there is some beautiful writing about Liz's pleasure in this baby). However, Liz's stepson, embarrassed, hopes she will not 'start on infantile sexuality', as he pokes the fire and 'the sparks fly upward.' We recognize here an embedded proverb, that man 'is born for trouble as the sparks fly upward'. Baby Cornelia will not, cannot, stay innocent. And psychoanalysis, which hopes to cure by enlightenment, cannot accommodate the psychopath; psychiatry, the voice of reason as a tool for understanding, has no answer to the passions.

The three women represent three intellectual disciplines, three aspects of culture. Liz represents medical science and psychiatry; Alix, English literature, though she knows a lot about Latin as well and reads history as well as poetry. Alix can distinguish Lucan the poet[2] from Lucan the murderer (Lord Lucan murdered his children's nanny in mistake for his wife and disappeared). Esther the art historian catalogues and interprets the iconography of a religion not her own, with wit and learning. Esther is interested in smiling, androgynous Saint Sebastians. Esther and her author must be aware, although neither of them mentions the fact, that suffering Saint Sebastians are a recognized form of homosexual sadistic pornography. Esther, like young Celia Harper, classical scholar, belongs with the detached intellectuals in Drabble's work, sexless, living for ideas: David Ollerenshaw, Hugo Mainwaring, Stephen Cox. Esther's research is sterile, she is sterile; her studies of such pictures as Guarino's Saint Agatha have taught her nothing about life. Esther too is a 'severed head' in the Iris Murdoch sense.[3] Her intellect is disengaged from her body, her emotions; Esther, the connoisseur of pictorial blood and torture, runs away when a real murder is committed in her block of flats. She has chosen a platonic love in an effort to avoid 'normal sexual intercourse', cannot cope when Claudio exhibits the irrational, the mark of the beast. There is not much of the rising sap of life in Esther. She is symbolized by her potted plant, which she thinks is dead and throws out. But the murderer Paul is wiser and knows that when palms look dead they are actually alive (resurrection symbolism, always important in Drabble). When Esther abandons Elena and returns to life in Britain, are we to understand she is renewed? Neither the art historian's nor the creative author's knowledge is adequate to explain the appalling pathology of everyday life. Today's atrocities link us with Lindow man and Tollund man (who are illustrated on the dust-jacket of the hardback edition). Both were early sacrificial victims, now preserved in museums. Celia Harper reads of atrocities in Tacitus, nibbling Kendal mint cake; eating equals survival, in Drabble's work: I eat, therefore I am alive and will survive.

Alix knows, at the start, that she has 'almost invented' Paul Whitmore. She is law-abiding and conscientious, yet she has always been 'peculiarly interested in prisons, discipline, conviction, violence and the criminal mentality. . . . Does her interest express her other darker, ever repressed self?' She wonders why she has spent so much of her adult life teaching in prisons, studying deviant behaviour. 'As though in a search for her own wholeness? Or in search of a refutation of the concept of original sin?'

Clearly, original sin is all around us and in our blindness we refuse to admit it is there.

Liz gets into hot water by arguing on television that a pair of lovers, under 16, should not have been persecuted; had they been left alone, the boy would not have committed suicide.

Reviewers misread this section. Lucy Ellmann in the *New Statesman and New Society*, 22 September 1989, wrote: 'Liz gets herself on telly as an advocate of sexual relationships with children. Her argument is a little hard to follow but would certainly make great TV.' Liz's argument is that the age of consent should be abolished, in the interests of young people: that teenage sex should be decriminalized. Liz says, 'I don't see what this case has to do with pederasty. . . . Or with paedophilia. It's more a Romeo and Juliet case. . . .' The politician sharing the TV programme says, 'But you can't deny that the removal of legal constraint would open the floodgates?' Liz's reply, cool, sensible, is 'You mean you think everyone is longing to have sex with the underaged, and that only the law prevents it?'

The politician does not answer her question, but goes on to talk about child abuse, child prostitution, child murder.

Liz's reply is that she does not think he's being logical. 'I'm not recommending that we decriminalise murder, or assault, or kidnapping, you know.' She asks another person:

> Do you really think that the desire of adults for sexual contact with children is so widespread and so strong that only the most severe social and legal sanctions can control it?

So far, so good. Then she sets the cat among the pigeons: 'And if this is so, does it ever occur to you that this desire itself could be less abnormal than you believe it to be? And possibly less harmful?'

This is not quite the same thing as recommending sex

between adults and children, though we learn eventually that Liz has enjoyed the attentions of dirty old men in Woolworth's as a child, before avoiding boys in adolescence to concentrate on her studies. Watching the TV programme, the family solicitor Clive Enderby knows more than Liz about her mysterious family: Liz has an illegitimate half-sister, Marcia, whose father was one of the aristocratic network from which has sprung Lady Henrietta Latchett, Charles Headleand's third wife. Rather improbably, Marcia's father has paid Rita Ablewhite a perpetual annuity so long as she keeps away. Has Rita been 'married off'? In real life, servant girls who became pregnant by their masters were dismissed without a character reference and usually bore their bastards in the workhouse. But this is a romance, a quest story. Marcia is explicitly a 'sister *ex machina*', a blatant device of plot.

Marcia's and Liz's younger sister Shirley has 'opened her legs' to her husband Cliff at 17, in a field, but after marriage has pursued a sporadic affair with Cliff's brother, Steve. Cliff has picked up an infection and has ceased relations with Shirley. When Shirley finds him dead in the car, poisoned by carbon monoxide fumes, she gets into her own car and drives for miles, right round the M25 road, which encircles London, and down to Dover. There she is picked up by a stranger called Robert (not to be confused with the aristocratic Minister for Culture, Robert Oxenholme, one of Henrietta's clan, who wants to marry Esther). Shirley's Robert offers her an idyll: he takes her to Paris, to the deserted flat of his faithless mistress, Amélie, and makes love to Shirley with a stamina remarkable in a man of his age. This would seem to be romantic for Shirley; Anita Brookner, reviewing the book in *The Spectator*, 30 September 1989, wrote:

> She has a lovely time with her Robert, the only sympathetic man in the book, and there is even a trace of Nancy Mitford in the way the adventure is described.

Brookner is alluding to Nancy Mitford's wish-fulfilment novel, *The Pursuit of Love*, in which Linda, after two failed marriages, finds passion as kept mistress of a sexy French Duke who knows all about clothes. Drabble's picture is more ironic, however, than Brookner gives her credit for: Robert is introduced as 'possibly' just a middle-aged philanderer, and this judgement is confirmed when Shirley leaves him (seemingly because the French plumbing is so bad). He has been using Shirley to revenge himself on Amélie. Shirley enjoys the soft womanly ache induced by prolonged love-making, but soon her stomach is upset and she has a 'strange stinging bloody vaginal discharge'. Robert has infected her with disease and is clearly one of Drabble's demon lovers, like Wyndham Farrar in *The Garrick Year,* James Otford in *The Waterfall* and Ted Stennet in *The Middle Ground.* Alix has always chosen 'safe' men, steering herself away from 'the bastard streak', but (it is implied) seeking vicarious excitement in her slightly prurient interest in Paul Whitmore. Even the title is ambiguous: Alix's curiosity is natural, in that everybody is interested in murders; but Paul himself is the 'curiosity' and however 'unnatural' we may call murder, history shows ritual killing, human sacrifice, to be so widespread, so recurrent, as to be, in some sense, natural.

Original sin is also a part of nature. Wild nature is cruel, violent, bloody and sexual. Fanny Kettle is the wife of an archaeologist. He has lost interest in sex, and thinks of her, amiably, as a nymphomaniac. Fanny shocks Susie Enderby, solicitor's wife, by her assumption that we are all promiscuous. Yet when Fanny holds a *Walpurgisnacht* party, Susie is introduced to Blake Leith, who we are told is a second-rate seducer, like someone out of a melodrama, and with him Susie launches into a passionate affair. Fanny has mixed a cocktail which may be aphrodisiac, or at any rate is intended to be; and Fanny's young son, Tony, ends up in bed with young Alice Enderby, whose black lace knickers decorate their bedpost: underage lovers, Romeo and Juliet again.

Drabble's attitude to sexual morality is not easy to interpret. Are we to agree that sex between consenting underage schoolchildren is natural and healthy, as Liz argues on television? Is Fanny a nature-goddess or a wicked witch? The point seems to be that the female party-giver, procuress, is either or both. Like mankind, nature itself is dual: Alix

> looks up to gaze at her snowdrops. They jostle in the wineglass on their thin stems. She lifts the face of one of them, gazes inquiringly into its intricate green and yellow and white,

and lets it fall back. With a sigh, the whole wineglassful rearranges itself, with inimitable once-only grace, to create a new pattern. The flowers shiver and quake into stillness. They cannot fall wrongly. They cannot make themselves into a false shape.

Alix is in the habit of singing hymns to herself as she drives through Yorkshire. The twin healers seem to be Wordsworthian nature and Christianity. The story ends with Brian finding inspiration to write another novel, the three friends on holiday in Italy. Alix has the last word on England:

> No . . . England's not a bad country. It's just a mean, cold, ugly, divided, tired, clapped-out post-imperial post-industrial slagheap covered in polystyrene hamburger cartons. It's not a bad country at all. I love it.

Jonathan Coe in the *Guardian* wrote:

> . . . these novels are plunged into a flaccid half-way house between the realistic and the symbolic, fatally clouding any relationship which they might have enjoyed with the world upon which they are supposed to be passing comment.

One might reasonably answer that one could say the same about the novels of, for instance, Dickens, not to mention more modern writers of fiction, though Coe is dismissive of Drabble's claim to be a 'Dickensian' novelist.

Miranda Seymour in the *Evening Standard* wrote:

> All the political and social trappings of the late Eighties are here—AIDS, Iranians, developers, statistical juggling. They are grafted on to the outmoded Hampstead Novel, the one Miss Drabble used to set in Kentish Town.
>
> The anger and despair are here in abundance. But they are old angers, old despairs, the depressing product of 20 years of an unrevised and seemingly immutable yearning for the ideal socialist state.

Considering the gentle satire on Brian Bowen for being an 'unreconstructed socialist', this seems wide of the mark. A month after the reviews appeared, John Ezard interviewed Drabble in the *Guardian* (14–15 October). Overall, in the reviews, said Ezard, 'the mood was to call time on the state-of-Britain novel and on techniques like authorial intervention.'

Drabble's reply, he reports, is that

> she is going to go on authorially intervening. Her postbag tells her most readers like it and academics love it. It's only a problem, she says, to critics who haven't caught up with Dickens, let alone John Fowles.

She added she knew why the reception had been

> a bit grim. It's a very peculiar, uncomfortable book. It's about how we cling on to normality in a world which at a national, international and personal level seems fairly odd these days. We live in this extreme world where continually we're made aware of extreme divisions within it. But the point is that we do manage to lead reasonably normal lives. And critics don't like the fact that people go on having pasta and a glass of wine while they're doing this. I did point out that it isn't about the state of Britain. But they never listen.

She also said:

> I'm not really as anti-Thatcher as I may seem. I do think something had to happen. Something undoubtedly had to be done about the unions, about the welfare dependency culture where the benefit structure was so complex that you needed an IQ of 2000 to understand it. The Labour government was borrowing money, you can't go on doing that. I agree with Mrs. Thatcher. I've never borrowed a penny in my life.
>
> But the wrong things were done. The problem was addressed with a kind of savagery and a misunderstanding of how people got into the muddle in the first place.

In an open letter published in the *Guardian*, 16 August 1990, she implored Mrs. Thatcher to visit the shabby parts of Britain.

> Unlike Prime Ministers and royalty I go to places that have not been cleaned up in anticipation of my arrival. . . . I would like to recommend that all Cabinet Ministers should take an unannounced, and if possible incognito, trip on public transport at least once a month. And it would be good if they were encouraged to wander on foot round some of the less picturesque corners of our towns and cities. Then go and have a look at Paris, or Geneva, or Venice, or Harare, or Toronto. Cities don't just spontaneously tidy themselves up. They need money, effort and, dare I say it, planning. . . .

She implores Mrs. Thatcher, the thrifty housewife, to spend money on maintenance.

Such decent concern can hardly be described as 'outdated'. Drabble is a novelist for our times. If she has been shamelessly autobiographical, she has found echoes, always, of deeper concerns. She exemplifies George Eliot's dictum that there is 'no private life which has not been determined by a wider public life.' And because she is a skilful entertainer, her sheer intellectual brilliance often goes unnoticed.

NOTES

1. Nora Foster Stovel, *Margaret Drabble: Symbolic Moralist*, p. 189.
2. Lucan (Marcus Annaeus Lucanus, A.D. 39–65). He was a Roman epic poet, forced to commit suicide because of his part in a conspiracy against the Roman emperor Nero. His ten-book epic on the civil war between Pompey and Julius Caesar is called the *Pharsalia*. Fanny Kettle's cocktail, which looks like methylated spirits, is called 'Pharsalian pink'.
3. Iris Murdoch (born 1919) has published more than twenty novels. *A Severed Head* was published in 1961. It is among the most famous of her novels and is about academics out of touch with their feelings.

12

A Writer's Britain (1979)

David Leon Higdon, an American, prefaces his book, *Shadows of the Past in Contemporary British Fiction*, with an observation: '. . . the English landscape struck me as being a palimpsest in which past, present and future co-exist, sometimes comfortably, sometimes uneasily.'[1] Coming from the barren wastes of the Western continent, he found our small, green island crowded with history. Those of us who live here take it for granted, particularly those of us with a literary education, who are conscious of Shakespeare's 'great creating nature', Wordsworth's idea of nature as therapeutic, of the impact made on the imagination of novelists by the Industrial Revolution: Benjamin Disraeli (1804–81), Charles Dickens (1812–70), Elizabeth Gaskell (1810–65), Charlotte Brontë (1816–55), D. H. Lawrence (1885–1930); of the opposition of town and country in the works of Jane Austen (1775–1817) and the references in the work of Thomas Hardy to Roman occupation and ancient gods. Behind Dickens lies the conflict between the views of Thomas Malthus (1766–1834) and Jeremy Bentham (1748–1832) on the one hand and those of Samuel Taylor Coleridge (1772–1834) and Thomas Carlyle (1795–1881) on the other. The conflict between the pragmatic Utilitarianism of Bentham and the vitalist, dynamic visions of Coleridge and Carlyle reverberate through the work of such novelists as Dickens, and are still resonating through Drabble's, as the nineteenth-century conflict between science and religion becomes a conflict between science and moral decisions on a human scale, between industry and environment. Other influential dichotomies are Matthew Arnold's opposition of 'Culture and anarchy',

'Hebraism and Hellenism'. Knowledge of the Bible and Shakespeare and Milton and Bunyan are no longer living popular culture, but those of us who went through the Cambridge English school in the '50s and '60s are rooted in them. American scholars tend to lack this background, or to hold it only sketchily. It is unnerving, for example, to find one 'Drabble scholar' solemnly thanking another for pointing out that the title of *The Millstone* is a reference to the Bible.[2] Drabble told Diana Cooper-Clark at interview:

> I read Bunyan at a very early age. And he profoundly affected my moral thinking, but I'm not alone in that. He profoundly affected the moral thinking of the whole of the seventeenth, eighteenth and nineteenth centuries. Everybody read *Pilgrim's Progress*. It was a way of looking at the world. It's like saying, 'Is the Bible irrelevant?' No, it's not. You may not believe it, but it's in your consciousness.[3]

The loss of religious faith that echoes through poets like Arnold (exemplified in his poem, 'Dover Beach'), Alfred Lord Tennyson and Thomas Hardy under the impact of Malthus and Charles Darwin (1809–82), author of *The Origin of Species*, is still felt as a lack in families where faith was held and, as we have seen, Drabble was influenced by 'fire and brimstone' religion. Literature is consoling for Drabble's characters: Frances Wingate the archaeologist, for instance, knows about 'Frost at Midnight'; Liz Headleand is well-read in English fiction and poetry; Emma Evans, like Drabble, thought Wordsworth dull at school, yet found his truths a revelation later on. And in the background lurks Drabble's awareness of John Stuart Mill's nervous breakdown at the age of 23 after a childhood where he was pressured into precocity; he cured it by reading Wordsworth. Such consciousness of Britain amounts to a map of the past, shared by Drabble and her Cambridge contemporaries. Drabble's works are essentially English in that they are informed by earlier literature, by history, Protestantism and eclecticism; as well as hostility to the influence of Leavis, she has expressed gratitude for what moulded us, and she exemplifies his ideal of culture: literate, liberal, humane. *A Writer's Britain* is the best gloss on her own works; it is also a fine and exhilarating work of commentary, original in form and distinguished in its own right.

For foreigners studying English literature, it is an invaluable tool. The magnificent photographs by Jorge Lewinski are keyed finely into the text, evoking present-day Britain together with the relics of its past. The book provides a learned and sensitive context for the study of English literature. It is full of curious learning: 'no man before Petrarch, the first Renaissance man, is known to have climbed a mountain for the sake of the view' [p. 18]. She explains that early religious settlements were sited where the monks would avoid the corruptions and ease of town life, not because of feeling for the countryside. She finds in medieval literature a pre-Romantic feeling for the damp and desolate. The sheer range of authors she quotes is astonishing. She is satirical about poems glorifying great houses where

> Workers and servants, in this ideal world, remain invisible . . . the country house of Uppark, where H. G. Wells's mother was housekeeper, was built with the servants' quarters landscaped out of sight, underground, because their intrusive presence would spoil the view. (p. 51)

All the quotations from writers are based securely on their life experience and circumstances, producing original insights. She writes with particular delicacy about poetry, comparing the rustic poet John Clare's 'Remembrances' with Wordsworth's better-known 'Immortality Ode', though adding that Robert Burns's range is wider than Clare's.

Crabbe and Cobbett are illuminated. She says it is impossible, within her allotted space, to 'do justice to the complexity and originality of Wordsworth's contribution to the literature of landscape'. He 'painted place as it had never been painted before, and connected it in new ways with man's thought processes and moral being' (p. 151). She admires Wordsworth for his *faith* . . . "that every flower enjoys the air it breathes" ' (p. 152). She suspects that Wordsworth drew such a response because

> he was drawing on deep sources of collective feeling, on a primitive animistic view of the world, certainly present

in earlier times, but powerfully suppressed by the scientific seventeenth and eighteenth centuries.

It is these unacknowledged 'collective feelings' that form the structural principle of *The Radiant Way* and *A Natural Curiosity*, though the emphasis is different from Wordsworth's; Wordsworth finds harmony, Drabble ferrets out danger.

She moves on to novelists such as George Eliot and Elizabeth Gaskell. Of ambivalence to industrial landscape, she writes that Wells, Huxley and Evelyn Waugh on the one hand

> condemn or question the advance of science, but at the same time they are enthralled by it, and cannot resist their admiration for a Brave New World of skyscrapers, aluminium furniture, glittering glass walls, aeroplanes and motorcars. A strange new beauty was growing out of the muddle, new forms, new aesthetic concepts, a new man-made paradise. Artists and architects responded more enthusiastically to this vision than writers, for obvious reasons, but writers could not fail to catch a glimmer of it. (p. 229)

Her own works reflect a similar ambivalence, the ambivalence of the twentieth century. She and I are agreed in finding the architecture of New York and Chicago exhilarating.

She adds that the love-hate relationship persists, though it is finding new objects.

> Suburban sprawl has become a new theme for poets and novelists, seen by some as a greater menace than the original industrial chaos. John Betjeman and Philip Larkin both write of strange unpoetic pockets of English life. . . . (p. 235)

We remember that Alix Bowen, in *The Radiant Way*, teaches Larkin's poem, 'They fuck you up, your mum and dad', to her class of female prisoners.

Drabble writes of poets and novelists who have written of London, sometimes of obscure districts where they lived. She includes diarists and autobiographers. On Virginia Woolf's anguish at having no more holidays in Cornwall after her mother died, and the transposition of those holidays to the Hebrides to create *To the Lighthouse*, Drabble writes:

> The landscape also changes, but far more slowly; it is a living link between what we were and what we have become. This is one of the reasons why we feel such profound and apparently

167

disproportionate anguish when a loved landscape is altered out of recognition; we lose not only a place, but a part of ourselves, a continuity between the shifting phases of our life. (p. 270)

A picture of the Frome Valley, Dorset, carries the caption, 'With Hardy each novel has its own world of landscape.' Drabble comments sadly that his poem 'In Time of "The breaking of Nations" ', which affirms the continuity of rural life ('this will go onward the same/ Though dynasties pass'), was mistaken: 'Change was sudden, irreversible, total . . . it is astonishing that so many landscapes of the past, described by writers, should still remain recognizable' [p. 98].

In a book she edited in 1976, *The Genius of Thomas Hardy*, she contributed an essay on 'Thomas Hardy and the Natural World'. In it she writes of *Tess of the D'Urbervilles*:

> Man and nature, the real and the symbolic, blend . . . in that . . . fine and famous passage in which Tess (who is after all only a milk maid) is seen as Eve in the first garden, in the 'spectral, half-compounded aqueous light' of early morning. The description of her meetings with Angel Clare, when they seem alone in a non-human world, with the summer fog lying on the meadows 'like a white sea, out of which the scattered trees rose like dangerous rocks', is one of the supreme passages of English literature. There is nothing prettily pastoral or intellectually inflated here, although the scene is a meadow, and Tess is compared to Eve, to Artemis, to Demeter. Man inhabits nature here in a way that no other writer I know has ever achieved, though some may have sensed it. John Clare sensed the union of man and nature, when he was a boy, but as a man he wrote of an Eden lost. Thomas Hardy re-creates Eden, and of all his many achievements as poet and novelist, this seems to me his greatest.[4]

This comment illuminates not only the genius of Hardy, but Drabble's own approach; in her work, too, the real and the symbolic are blended, as she struggles to re-create an Eden in the slagheap which is still, in some respects, England's green and pleasant land.

NOTES

1. David Leon Higdon, *Shadows of the Past in Contemporary British Fiction* (London: Macmillan, 1984), p. ix. Contains a useful chapter on *The Realms of Gold*, pp. 152–68.
2. Matthew, 18:6; Mark, 9:42; Luke, 17:2.
3. Interview with Diana Cooper-Clark, *Atlantic Monthly*, 246, No. 5 (November 1980), 69–75. Reprinted in Ellen Cronan Rose (ed.), *Critical Essays*, pp. 22–3.
4. Margaret Drabble, *The Genius of Thomas Hardy*, p. 181.

Selective Bibliography

CAMPBELL, JANE, and DOYLE, JAMES, (eds.), *The Practical Vision: Essays in Honour of Flora Roy* (Waterloo, Ontario: Wilfred Laurier University Press, 1978)

CREIGHTON, JOANNE V., *Margaret Drabble* (London: Methuen, 1985)

DRABBLE, MARGARET, 'Virginia Woolf—a Personal Debt', originally in *Harpers Bazaar and Queen*, September 1972, pp. 90–1, 128. (Reprinted in limited edition by Aloe Editions, 1973)

——— *The Genius of Thomas Hardy* (London: Weidenfeld & Nicolson, 1976)

——— *A Writer's Britain* (London: Thames & Hudson, 1979)

——— *The Tradition of Women's Fiction: Lectures in Japan*, ed. Yukako Suga (Tokyo: Oxford University Press, 1982)

HANNAY, JOHN, *The Intertextuality of Fate: A Study of Margaret Drabble* (Columbia: University of Missouri Press, 1986)

KENYON, OLGA, *Women Novelists Today: A Survey of English Writing in the Seventies and Eighties* (Brighton: Harvester, 1988)

——— *Women Writers Talk: Interviews with 10 Women Writers* (Oxford: Lennard Publishing, 1989)

MORAN, MARY HURLEY, *Margaret Drabble: Existing Within Structures* (Carbondale: Southern Illinois University Press, 1983)

MYER, VALERIE, GROSVENOR, *Margaret Drabble: Puritanism and Permissiveness* (London: Vision Press; New York, Barnes & Noble, 1974)

——— Recorded Interview, RI 2007, British Council, 1977

ROSE, ELLEN CRONAN, *Equivocal Figures: The Novels of Margaret Drabble* (London: Macmillan; New York: Barnes & Noble, 1980).

——— (ed.) *Critical Essays on Margaret Drabble* (Boston: G. K. Hall, 1985)

ROXMAN, SUSANNA, *Guilt and Glory: Studies in Margaret Drabble's Novels 1963–80* (Stockholm: Almqvist & Wiksell International, 1984)

SADLER, LYNN VEACH, *Margaret Drabble* (Boston: Twayne, 1986)

SCHMIDT, DOREY, (ed.), *Margaret Drabble: Golden Realms* (Edinburg: Pan American University School of Humanities, Living Author Series 4, 1982).

STOVEL, NORA FOSTER, *Margaret Drabble: Symbolic Moralist* (Mercer Island: Starmont Contemporary Writers series, 1989)

Index

171

Index